A ROSE FOR MRS. LINCOLN

Mary Todd Lincoln by Katherine Helm. *White House Collection.*

A Rose for Mrs. Lincoln

A Biography of Mary Todd Lincoln

By DAWN LANGLEY SIMMONS

BEACON PRESS   BOSTON

Copyright © 1970 by Dawn Langley Simmons
Library of Congress catalog card number: 68–24369
International Standard Book Number: 0–8070–5448–2
Beacon Press books are published under the auspices
of the Unitarian Universalist Association
Published simultaneously in Canada by Saunders of Toronto, Ltd.
All rights reserved
Printed in the United States of America

Edgar Lee Masters, "Ann Rutledge," from *Spoon River Anthology*, by Edgar Lee Masters, copyrighted 1914, 1915, 1916, 1942 by Edgar Lee Masters, reprinted with permission of Mrs. Ellen C. Masters.
The letters by Mrs. Abraham Lincoln to Mr. Alphonse Donn are reprinted by courtesy of the National Park Service.

*A wedding gift
for my husband*
JOHN-PAUL SIMMONS
*St. Clement's Church
Hastings, England
November 9, 1969*

CONTENTS

	Author's Note vii
One	The Girl with the Bluish-Gray Eyes 1
Two	For Eternity 17
Three	Married Life 25
Four	Washington at Last 38
Five	A Death in the Family 54
Six	Circuit Days 61
Seven	A Wish Come True 68
Eight	Wife of the President-Elect 74
Nine	Life in the White House 92
Ten	The First Family 100
Eleven	War Days 107
Twelve	The Republican Queen 115
Thirteen	Critics and the Family 119
Fourteen	Willie 127
Fifteen	A Dragon for a Champion 137
Sixteen	Emilie's Visit 143
Seventeen	A Second Term 148
Eighteen	A President Passes 154
Nineteen	The Exile 165
Twenty	Tad 181
	Selected Bibliography 195

ILLUSTRATIONS

Mary Todd Lincoln by Katherine Helm.   *Frontispiece*

The Lincoln House, Springfield, Illinois.   28

Interior of the Lincoln House, Springfield, Illinois.   51

Mrs. Abraham Lincoln and her sons, William and Thomas.   75

Elizabeth Keckley, Mary Todd Lincoln's dressmaker, confidante, and friend.   87

Abraham Lincoln and his son, Tad.   96

Mary Todd Lincoln.   108

Abraham Lincoln.   123

The Lincoln bedroom at the White House as it is today.   158

The Tomb of Abraham and Mary Todd Lincoln, Springfield, Illinois.   164

Robert Lincoln.   185

AUTHOR'S NOTE

My acquaintance with Mary Todd Lincoln, wife of the Sixteenth President of the United States, began long ago during my childhood in rural England. Then, during the summer holidays, it was my job of a Sunday afternoon to bear that all-important envelope containing his weekly *Observer* book review from Sissinghurst Castle to the village mailbox for Sir Harold Nicolson. The following week I always made it my business to read what he had said, although my youthful mind wasn't always able to understand him.

One review in particular stuck in my mind. He had been given a scathing biography of a certain Mary Todd Lincoln to review and, although a compassionate man himself, on the strength of what he read Sir Harold felt bound to call Mrs. Lincoln "a very silly woman."

In such ways are born the ideas for future books. Sir Harold and his talented wife Vita (V. Sackville-West) both encouraged me with my writing, teaching me discipline and the joy of research. My own research for *A Rose for Mrs. Lincoln* took me to far places, both here in the United States and abroad.

I would particularly like to thank the following for help and encouragement:

Mrs. Lyndon B. Johnson; Mrs. Elizabeth Carpenter, Staff Director to Mrs. Johnson at the White House; James T. Hickey, Curator, Lincoln Collection, Illinois State Historical Society; Mrs. Paul M. Rhymer, Curator of Prints, Chicago Historical Society; Clyde C. Walton, State Historian, Illinois State Historical Society and William K. Alderfer, also of the library; the Library of Congress; the New York Public Library; Geneva B. Pullen, Reference Librarian, Lexington Public Library, Lexington, Kentucky; Miss

Author's Note : : *page* x

Virginia Rugheimer, Librarian, and her staff at the Charleston Library Society, Charleston, South Carolina, and in particular Mrs. Minnie Pringle Haigh for obtaining me many rare books; Marion Wefer for her notes on Elizabeth Keckley; Virgie Morgan; Margaret Rummel; Belle Donnelly Hayes; Verona Florentine Adams; Kim Andrews; H. Reid, Carolinas Editor, *Times-Herald*, Newport News, Virginia; Florrie Reese; Barbara van Kampen; Valaria Gittens; Isabelle Angus; Gwendoline Martha Ticehurst Burgess; Paul Myers, Curator, Theater Collection, Library and Museum of The Performing Arts, the New York Public Library at Lincoln Center, New York, and Dorothy L. Swerdlove, his first assistant; and my typists, Gladys Fletcher of Charleston, South Carolina, and Gertrude Young of Worcester, England.

CHAPTER ONE

THE GIRL WITH THE BLUISH-GRAY EYES

The girl with the bluish-gray eyes watched solemnly as the gang of Negroes, men, women, and even children, shuffled slowly by the front door of her home on Main Street in Lexington. Manacled two abreast, and connected by a long length of chain, the unfortunate creatures were passing through Kentucky en route to the cotton fields of Georgia or the distant rice plantations of Louisiana.

With her cousin Elizabeth Humphreys, young Mary Todd witnessed such scenes frequently and both knew that Sally, the family conscience and their adored nurse, had chalked a mark on the back fence so that any runaway slave headed for the Ohio River and freedom could expect some "vittles" to sustain him.

Elizabeth was Mary's confidante, having joined the Todd household in order to better her education in the fine schools of Lexington. They shared the same room, the same secrets and interests. After reading in a New Orleans newspaper of a certain Madame La Laurie's cruelty to the Negroes she owned, Elizabeth recorded, "We were horrified and talked of nothing else for days. If one such case could happen, it damned the whole institution." Elizabeth Humphreys also speaks of happier things, such as the walks they enjoyed in the Todds' spacious garden, of the lemon-verbena, the buster-pinks and, in particular, the roses. "Mary," wrote Elizabeth, "even as a child always loved to wear flowers in her hair." Of these, roses were her favorite.

At eight, Mary, who had been born in Lexington, December 13, 1818, had entered the academy of Dr. John Ward, in a large two-story building located at the southwest corner of Market and Second Streets. Born in Connecticut, Dr. Ward had been Bishop of North Carolina before migrating for health reasons to Kentucky. At Lexington, in addition to serving as rector of fashionable Christ Church, he had started his school which, with his advanced views on co-education, was unusual. Kind and scholarly, he was at the same time a firm disciplinarian. His belief in early morning recitation was to develop in Mary Todd a most retentive memory that would serve her well in the years to come. Dr. Ward was also in favor of starting work very early and classes began at 5:00 A.M. Says Elizabeth,

> His requirements and rules were very strict and woe to her who did not conform to the letter. Mary accepted the conditions cheerfully, even eagerly, and never came under his censure. Mr. Ward required his pupils to recite some of their lessons before breakfast. On bright summer mornings this was no hardship, and Mary skipped blithely to her recitations, but she never murmured when conditions were not pleasant. When she had to get up out of her warm bed and dress by candle-light, she smiled and trudged sturdily through snow and sleet. . . . Mary was far in advance over girls of her age in education. She had a retentive memory and a mind that enabled her to grasp and thoroughly understand the lessons she was required to learn. It was a hard task but long before I was through mine she had finished hers and was plying her knitting-needles. We were required to knit ten rounds of socks every evening.

Some years before, as a small child, Mary's special friend had been a little boy with black hair and gray eyes. Determination to succeed in everything he did, even then, seemed to mark the course of his life, for John Cabell Breckenridge would grow up to be Vice President of the United States and, what was more ironic, a Presidential candidate against Mary's future husband.

Two blocks away, at Transylvania University, young Jefferson Davis attended his studies. In years to come, as leader of the Confederacy, he would also oppose Mary's husband.

The Girl with the Bluish-Gray Eyes : : *page 3*

Mary Todd's grandfather, Levi Todd, formerly of Providence Township, Pennsylvania, was one of the party of hunters who, sitting around their campfire on a warm June night, gave Lexington its name. The log cabins built by such sturdy pioneer settlers had long since been replaced by more stately homes, for Lexington had thrived so well that in Mary's day men called it the Athens of the West.

Levi Todd's ancestors were stubborn Scottish Covenanters, who, not being in agreement with the Established Church of England, had fled their heather-strewn heath for the North of Ireland, later emigrating to America. On February 25, 1779, in the fort located at St. Asaph's in Lincoln County, Kentucky, Levi married Jane Briggs. He founded Todd's Station, becoming clerk of the first court held in what was then considered the West.

Coming to Lexington in 1780, Levi was one of the first to buy land upon which to build his home. Appointed first clerk of the Fayette County Court, he held this position of trust until his death. As with most of the early pioneers he became involved with many military operations, at one time succeeding the now-legendary Colonel Daniel Boone as Commander of the Kentucky Militia.

Later, General Levi Todd, as he was locally known, raised eleven children at Ellerslie, his beautiful home near Lexington. His seventh child, Robert Smith Todd, born on February 25, 1791, was Mary Todd's father.

Robert fell in love with seventeen-year-old Eliza Parker, a lively, pretty girl with a calm, happy disposition. Her father, the late Major Robert Parker, had been a Revolutionary officer and was a first cousin of Levi Todd. Her mother, Elizabeth, was the eldest daughter of General Andrew Porter, a friend of George Washington.

Widow Parker was to be a strong influence upon the life of her granddaughter Mary. She had no opposition to her own daughter Eliza's courtship with Robert Todd, which was briefly interrupted by the War of 1812. Eliza was on hand to wave goodbye as her fiancé, now Private Todd, marched down Short Street with his colleagues in the Lexington Light Infantry wearing "brilliant uniforms of blue, with red facings, bell-buttons and jaunty red cockades floating from their black hats." He was soon to return, somewhat embarrassed at having nearly succumbed, not from wounds honorably received in battle, but from an attack of pneumonia! Upon recovering he wed the "sprightly" Eliza before returning to the army next day. In 1813 Robert S. Todd returned home to Lexington where his young wife was waiting. There they commenced married life in a comfortable house built on a lot belonging to the Widow Parker, which was next to her own home on Short Street.

Robert and Eliza's married life is scantily recorded. In a few short years Eliza became the mother of several children. Her elder daughters, Elizabeth and Frances, were followed by a son called Levi after his noted grandfather. On December 13, 1818, Eliza gave birth to her third daughter, naming her Mary Ann.

Mary Ann's father, though described as being "impetuous, high-strung and nervous," was nevertheless a good businessman and provider for his young family. On December 6, 1817, Robert joined another veteran of the recent war, Sergeant Bird Smith, formerly of Trotter's Cavalry, as a partner in what they described as an "Extensive Grocery Establishment" at Cheapside. It was announced in the local *Gazette* that a member of the firm would personally attend "foreign markets by which they will be enabled to supply their customers with every article in their line, on better terms and of better quality—indeed with any articles, such as fruits, *et cetera* that heretofore could not be procured." Smith and Todd, as the new enterprise was known, were firm believers in advertising their wares in the local newspaper.

Eliza, who scarcely seemed to have time to recover fully from one pregnancy before another baby was on the way, was fortunate in having a number of devoted house servants to help her run her home and look after the infant children.

Two years later Robert Parker Todd was born, to survive only two years. According to Lexington custom, Nelson, the body servant, drove off in the family barouche, carrying black-bordered funeral tickets which he left at the homes of family friends. Each ticket read,

Yourself and family are invited to attend the funeral of Robert P. Todd, infant son of Mr. R. S. Todd, from his

The Girl with the Bluish-Gray Eyes : : *page 5*

residence on Short Street, this evening at 5 o'clock.
Lexington. July 22, 1822.

When she was six years old, Mary was thrilled when another sister arrived. She was named Ann Maria after one of Robert S. Todd's sisters and so Mary Ann became Mary.

The following year Lexington celebrated the Fourth of July with Major General Winfield Scott, hero of the Battle of Chippewa, attending as guest of honor.

Although the new Secretary of State, Henry Clay, contemporarily described as being "inflexible to ill, and obstinately just," and Major General Scott highlighted the celebrations, the Todd and Parker families were noticeably absent. That day another son, George Rogers Clark Todd, had been born into the house on Short Street. His arrival had cost the young mother her life. In the Widow Parker's house opposite, the small Todd children, at least those old enough to understand, had been peeping through closed shutters all day watching the many comings and goings in their own home. Dr. Ben Dudley and Dr. Elisha Warfield had done their best to save Eliza, but to no avail. Once more Nelson drove off to deliver the funeral tickets.

Yourself and family are respectfully invited to attend the funeral of Mrs Eliza P., Consort of Robert S. Todd, Esq., from his residence on Short Street, this Evening at 4 o'clock.
July 6, 1825.

They buried her beside little Robert in a cemetery on Main Street. Later their bodies were removed to the new Todd family lot in Lexington Cemetery.

In an age when childbirth mortality was high, Robert Smith Todd found himself a widower at thirty-four with six young children to care for, the youngest being only a few days old. Mary was then six-and-a-half, an impressionable age. The placid, cheerful disposition of her mother was replaced by that of her emotional and sensitive father. Such a difference was bound to influence her life.

When, a few months later, Robert S. Todd was already courting the comely Elizabeth Humphreys, the Widow Parker was much incensed. Elizabeth, better known as Betsy, was the daughter of Dr. Alexander Humphreys. A member of a prominent Kentucky family, she was a young woman of charm and culture. She had first met Robert at Frankfort in January, 1826, when, having again been named clerk of the Lower House, he was attending the opening of the General Assembly.

The young widower was immediately attracted to the educated Betsy, who could boast a number of distinguished relatives, including her three uncles: Preston and Samuel Brown, both physicians of renown, the latter having earned the distinction of being the first professor of medicine at Transylvania University; and Senator James Brown of Louisiana, who later became the United States Minister to France.

While he was a widower, Robert's sister Eliza (Mrs. Charles M. Carr) advised him on the care of his little ones, while an unmarried sister-in-law, Ann Maria Parker, moved over from her mother's house opposite to take charge of the household. Her task was lightened by the presence of the house servants, slaves who had been brought up with the family; Chaney, the cook; Nelson, the coachman and body servant; and Jane Saunders, the housekeeper. Nelson, in addition to looking after the stables, served at table and was entrusted with the marketing. "Ruling" everybody was Sally, the nurse, assisted by her young helpmate, Judy.

Eliza's mother was very outspoken in her condemnation of the match between her son-in-law and Betsy Humphreys, and Robert saw fit to write his future wife, then visiting in New Orleans, warning her of the unpleasant situation.

> You have no doubt observed with what avidity and
> eagerness an occasion of this kind is seized hold of for the
> purpose of detraction and to gratify personal feelings of
> ill-will and indeed often times how much mischief is done
> without any bad motive. May I be permitted to put you on
> your guard against persons of this description. Not that
> I would wish to stifle fair enquiry, for I feel in the review
> of my past life a consciousness that such would not
> materially affect me in your estimation, although there are

many things which I have done and said, I would wish had never been done—and such I presume is the case of every one disposed to be honest with himself. . . .

Late in October he again wrote Betsy, to whom he was now engaged, begging her quickly to arrange their wedding.

> I hope you will not consider me importunate in again urging upon your consideration the subject of my last letter. I am sure if you knew my situation, you would not hesitate to comply with my wishes in fixing a day for our marriage in this or the early part of the ensuing week.

Betsy was willing and on Wednesday, November 1, 1826, she married Robert Smith Todd in her parents' beautiful home at Frankfort. The newlyweds returned to Lexington, and their house which was next door to the home of widow Parker.

The Lexington in which Mary Todd spent her childhood was a pleasant, well-to-do town noted for its many trees and shrubs. To the stranger there was an air of wealth about the spacious homes built, it seemed, more for comfort than for show. Inside they were tastefully furnished as befitted the well-educated families that inhabited them.

> There is nothing of the bustle and noise and squeeze of Louisville, nor anything resembling the compact squares and busy crowds of Cincinnati, but we see quiet streets, shaded by long rows of locusts; old mansions surrounded by venerable trees, and modern edifices of unostentatious beauty embowered in shrubbery.

So read a contemporary description in the *Western Monthly*. Visitors compared Lexington favorably with other flourishing cities, particularly noting the "gaiety" of the number of gigs, barouches, and coaches of all shapes and sizes that were seen on the streets from morning to night. They were particularly numerous in the cool of the afternoon when the ladies of the town enjoyed taking their rides. In fact there were so many carriages that a writer dubbed Lexington "the city that goes on wheels."

Of the people themselves—and this is interesting, in view of Mary Todd's later experiences as First Lady in Washington, when society erroneously expected an uneducated woman from the backwoods—a contemporary noted, "The inhabitants are as polished and, I regret to add, as luxurious as those of Boston, New York or Baltimore, and their assemblies and parties are conducted with as much ease and grace as in the oldest towns in the Union." According to Mary Todd's niece, Katherine Helm, "the town was filled to overflowing with academical, medical, and law students drawn from all over the middle West and South." The Lexington newspapers led the press of the state while the Lexington bar was said to be the strongest in the United States.

The Todd home continually entertained the finest minds in the city, which left their mark on Mary, the impressionable little girl destined to marry one of the great men of history. She was fearless, something of a tomboy, and certainly not shy, as the story of an early encounter with Henry Clay testifies. At the age of thirteen she galloped off on her pony to visit Ashland, Clay's lovely home, where she boldly announced to the butler that she wished to see the famed orator immediately. When the butler later returned with the news that Clay begged to be excused because he had important guests, the child replied, "I can't help that. I've come all the way out to Ashland to show Mr. Clay my new pony. You go right back and tell him that Mary Todd would like him to step out here for a moment."

Clay capitulated, hurrying out to the driveway followed by his guests, who were much amused when Miss Todd declared, "Mr. Clay, my father says you are the best judge of horseflesh in Fayette County. What do you think about this pony?" After Henry Clay had praised her animal, Mary was invited inside for dinner, where she thoroughly enjoyed the political conversation. Once she even interrupted to say, "Mr. Clay, my father says you will be the next President of the United States. I wish I could go to Washington and live in the White House." Some of the guests expressed agreement while Mary confessed, "I begged my father to be President but he only laughed and said he would rather see you there than to be President himself. He must like you more than he does himself." Then she added, "My father is a very, very peculiar man, Mr. Clay. I don't think he really wants to be President." Clay smiled and promised her a special visit to the White House should he ever attain such an honor. Mary quickly accepted the premature invitation, but not before announcing, "If you were not already married, I would wait for you."

It was not long before Robert S. Todd and his second wife started their family, the first baby arriving in 1827. After that, eight others would appear with clockwork regularity. Little wonder that Elizabeth Humphreys, Mary's friend, recalled in later years that "Aunt [Betsy, another Elizabeth Humphreys] was very delicate and I often wonder how she lived through some of those years."

By 1832 Betsy had become the mother of four infants, one of whom died, so that there were nine children altogether in the home. With all the house servants, visitors, and general bustle, the Todd household could not be called a placid establishment. Mary had little individual attention except perhaps from Sally, the nurse, who on Sundays attended the white folks' church, sitting regally up in the Negroes' gallery. Afterwards she came home to find fault with everything that Judy, the under-nurse, had done in her absence. Then she lectured the older children on their shortcomings and what Ol' Man Satan would do if he caught them. The culprits would feel the glare of Sally's "stern, accusing eye" as she reprimanded them for all their "sins" of the week before.

Sally's simple religious faith was not lost on Mary. Once when she was visiting her Aunt Carr at Walnut Hills a band of poor Indians appeared. The other children with whom she was playing rushed to find hiding places, for all had been brought up on gory tales of pioneer settlers and Indians. Everybody was hidden but Mary, whose legs seemed turned to stone. Thinking of Sally she began to cry, "Hide me, oh, my Savior, hide me." As it turned out, the visiting Indians were friendly. All they wanted was some free food and clothing.

Elizabeth tells us that Mary enjoyed sewing, being the only Todd daughter to acquire skill in the use of a needle and thread. Even Betsy, her stepmother, could not sew, although she did crochet and knit, teaching her daughters and stepdaughters how to do so too. So adept was Mary with a needle that when her father returned from a visit to New Orleans with dolls that squeaked for her and Elizabeth, Mary was able to make their clothes. She was also permitted by Betsy to tell the sewing woman what kind of dresses to cut from the embroidered pink muslin that Robert Todd had brought the two girls from his trip.

These dresses made up for the disappointment their pride had suffered when, longing to have grown-up hoop skirts, they had begged willow switches from a neighbor. With these Mary constructed two awkward apparatuses that bulged in all directions from beneath their best dresses. They were just off to Sunday School at McChord Church when Betsy caught them. Mary, ten years old, burst into a flood of tears which, considering all the work she had put into the improvised hoop skirts, was not surprising. Elizabeth reports that for years afterward "this escapade was a standing joke in the family."

The discord between Mary's grandmother, the Widow Parker, and Mary's father and stepmother could not have been pleasant, especially as the children of the first marriage were frequent visitors to the house across the way. Little wonder that Eliza's children grew up with an undercurrent of ill-feeling for their stepmother Betsy. So unhappy was the situation that, in 1832, Robert wisely removed his household to a double brick house on Main Street, the choice of which was influenced by its beautiful formal garden filled with flowering shrubs and bulbs. Betsy was passionately fond of flowers. The new garden also boasted a little stream, the Town Fork of Elkhorn Creek, in which, on hot summer days, the children could wade, float paper boats, and chase the minnows. To the left of the house, a conservatory, so fashionable at that time, opened onto a shady white gravel walk.

That same year Mary's older sister Elizabeth, who had only recently been a bridesmaid when her close friend Mary Jane Warfield had married Cassius Marcellus Clay, wed Ninian W. Edwards, son of Governor Ninian Edwards of Illinois, on February 18. She was only sixteen at the time, and the bridegroom was a junior at

Transylvania. Records of the nuptials are brief, for this was an age when a true lady's name only appeared in print when she was married and when she died. Consequently the *Kentucky Reporter* recorded in its issue of February 29, 1832,

> Married in this city, Ninian W. Edwards of Illinois, to Miss Elizabeth Todd, daughter of Robert S. Todd, Esq.

After graduating in 1833 from Transylvania, young Ninian took his child-bride to Illinois, where she became the mistress of his widower father's home.

That same year Mary, then fourteen, became a boarder at the most fashionable finishing school in Lexington, an establishment presided over by Madame Victorie Charlotte Le Clere Mentelle.

Early on Monday mornings, the patriarchal Nelson, Robert Todd's coachman, drove Mary to school, fetching her home again on Friday afternoons. Boarding, washing, and tuition cost one hundred and twenty dollars a year.

The next four years were to be among the happiest of her life. Both Victorie and her husband, Augustus Waldemare Mentelle, were born in Paris. The only child of a physician, Mme. Mentelle's mother had died when her daughter was very small. Her physician father is described in Mme. Mentelle's obituary in the *Kentucky Statesman*, September 14, 1860 (she lived almost to complete her 90th year), as being "engaged in a large and laborious practice" and of raising her as he would have done a son, "treating her with such sternness and rigor as to leave in her heart no pleasant memories of her childhood." On one occasion he subjected her to his own theory of how to conquer the fear of death, by locking her up all night in a room containing the corpse of a close acquaintance!

Waldemare Mentelle was the son of a historiographer to the King of France. Shortly after the Mentelles' marriage they were forced to flee the French Revolution. Emigrating to America, they settled first at Gallipolis, Ohio, in 1793. About 1795 they moved to Washington in Mason County, Kentucky, finally arriving at Lexington in 1798, where for some years they taught dancing and French. Later they formed their own boarding school for girls in a house located opposite Henry Clay's beloved Ashland on Richmond Pike. It was put at their disposal by the owner, Mary Todd's cousin, Mary Owen Russell, widow of Colonel James Russell, and daughter of Colonel John Todd who was killed at the Battle of Blue Licks in 1782. The Mentelles gave it the beautiful name of Rose Hill.

It was under the influence of this charming, intellectual Frenchwoman, who in her own lifetime was described as being "a woman equalled, never excelled," that young Mary Todd came. Due to Mme. Mentelle's skill Mary became fluent in French and, says Elizabeth Humphreys,

> She never gave it up, but as long as I knew her continued to read the finest French authors. At different times, French gentlemen came to Lexington to study English and when one was fortunate enough to meet her, he was not only surprised, but delighted to find her perfect acquaintance with the language.

According to Elizabeth it was also at the Mentelles' that Mary learned to dance so gracefully. "In after years," says Elizabeth, "it was her favorite amusement and the aristocratic society of Lexington afforded ample opportunity for the indulgence of this pastime." However, dancing and French were not by any means the only subjects taught at this fashionable finishing school. On March 6, 1838, the Lexington *Intelligencer* carried an advertisement concerning the Mentelles' establishment, declaring that it gives "a truly useful and solid English education in all its branches."

Remembering her own Spartan childhood, and not wishing to impose such hardships on the girls left in her charge, Mme. Mentelle allowed them plenty of recreation after the afternoon classes were over. On fine days they were encouraged to take long walks through the wooded grounds and read aloud to each other in the open air. Mary and her fellow students often had the opportunity to wave greetings to her old friend, Mr. Clay, now affectionately

The Girl with the Bluish-Gray Eyes : : page 13

known as "The Great Commoner," as he drove into Lexington to collect his mail.

As they were not allowed to receive visitors, the students were allowed other compensations, such as dancing on a wintry evening to the music of the violin, gaily played by the aging M. Mentelle. Mme. Mentelle and her two accomplished daughters instructed the girls "in the latest and most fashionable Cotillions, Round & Hop Waltzes, Hornpipes, Galopades, Mohawks, Spanish, Scottish, Polish, Tyrolienne dances and the beautiful Circassian Circle."

As educators for Mary Todd, the Mentelles were a fortunate choice, for unconsciously they were fitting her for a life in high places. As for her prowess in French, not only would her reading of current French novels give her special social status, but a fluent use of the language itself would later prove to be invaluable.

Meanwhile, at home, Robert Todd had engaged a tutor to cope with the education of some of his younger children. This tutor was an Episcopalian student of theology whom Mary found to be very incompatible. The more she tried to be agreeable to the touchy young man, the more suspicious he became that she was making fun of him. Observed Elizabeth, "He waged a war without cause."

With her father often away on business, and her stepmother confined to her room by reason of exhaustion, the two adversaries found themselves at weekends eating at the same table with nobody to control the trend of their conversation. Wrote the embarrassed boarder, Elizabeth,

> One morning on such an occasion Mary and I went to the breakfast room. Mary took her seat at the head of the table and Mr.———, the young tutor, took the seat at the foot, I on the other side. Grace was said with due reverence and then we commenced with keen appetites on the feast of good things before us. We had some remarkably fine maple syrup. Mary helped me and offered some to Mr.——— with the remark that she understood the Yankees always ate molasses with everything. It was the word "Yankee," I suppose, that raised the storm. He was greatly irritated. With a black frown and rolling his R's

more than usual, he spoke with great emphasis. "Miss Mary," he said, "there is a point beyond endurance which I cannot and will not stand."

Mary was, you must remember, one of a large family of boys and girls who jested much and seized on the slightest pretext to tease each other unmercifully. The young tutor looked so fierce and his wrath so great to have been occasioned by such a small amount of teasing, and the scene so ludicrous to Mary that she leaned back in her chair and laughed so merrily and contagiously that even Mr.———'s anger was dissipated and he joined in our laughter. The laughter acted like a charm and the rest of that day we three sailed on a calm sea of good humor.

Mary joined the rest of the family for their annual short vacation at Crab Orchard Springs, Kentucky, a resort patronized by the wealthy residents of the state, and where Betsy had been ordered to take the health-giving waters. For Mary, the bustling preparations were almost as exciting as the stay itself. Sally and her cohorts placed white covers over the sofas and chairs in the fine double parlors; piles of little white muslin dresses were stacked high on the fourposter beds ready for packing. Only the older boys, thinking themselves too old for such frivolous excursions, elected to stay at home.

For Mary, Crab Orchard Springs was a welcome interlude in her studious life for there were many old friends to greet. Evenings were filled with music and dancing; the Negro fiddlers played their gay airs by candlelight. There were belles and beaux, husbands and wives, old folks and their grandchildren. Crab Orchard Springs was a nostalgic, magic place, and afterwards Mary returned pleasantly refreshed to her studies at Mme. Mentelle's.

Mary spent weekends at home with other young people her age. Although she had entrée to the most aristocratic Bluegrass families, she did not give her heart to any of their sons. Says Cousin Elizabeth rather bluntly, "She accepted their attentions but at times her face indicated a lack of interest."

In Lexington Mary Todd was never more than a sub-debutante,

The Girl with the Bluish-Gray Eyes : : page 15

for her real entry into society was yet to begin in far-off Springfield, Illinois. However, Mary patronized Mathurin Giron's unique ballrooms, the most fashionable in Kentucky with their Tuscan pilasters outside, along with other young Lexington bluebloods. On the first floor of Giron's was the French confectionery that Mary had known from childhood, and where the enormous "castellated" cake decorated with sugared red, white, and blue stripes had been lovingly baked for the visit of the aging Marquis de Lafayette in 1825. Here as a little girl Mary had often shopped for meringues and macaroons, at the same time forming an enduring friendship with Mathurin Giron, the proprietor, only five feet tall and plump. Later she was able to try out her newly-learned French in his critical presence.

Perhaps one of the most exciting days in all Mary's life was when she and Cousin Elizabeth were permitted to go with Grandmother Humphreys, Betsy's mother, to a ball in Frankfort. Mrs. Humphreys, described as being "exquisite" in dress, mind, and manner, represented something of an ideal to Mary, who vowed to emulate her. On the occasion of the ball, the two girls watched admiringly as Grandmother, then seventy-three years old, wearing a satin gown and lace cap especially imported from France, confidently led the grand march.

This Grandmother Humphreys died when her step-granddaughter, Mary, was only eighteen, but she had further influenced Mary Todd's view on slavery. Grandmother Humphreys's will made provision to free all those slaves who had faithfully served her. The will read in part,

> In the name of God Amen: I, Mary Humphreys, of the town of South Frankfort, and County of Franklin and State of Kentucky, do make and ordain this my last will and testament. . . .
>
> 9th. I devise my negro slave, John Wales, unto my son, David C. Humphreys, until the Twenty-fifth day of December, Eighteen Hundred and Forty, on which said day the said John Wales is to be free and emancipate from all kind of servitude.
>
> 10th. I devise my negro girl, Jane, to my daughter,

Elizabeth Todd, until the Twenty-fifth day of December, Eighteen Hundred and Forty-four, on which said date the said Jane is to be free from all kind of servitude and should the said Jane have any children before the day on which she is to be free, the said child or children, if boys are hereby devised to the said Elizabeth L. Todd until they respectively attain the age of twenty-eight years, whereby they are to be free and emancipate from all manner of servitude; if girls they are hereby devised to the said Elizabeth L. Todd until they respectively attain the age of twenty-one years, when they and any increase they may have are to be free and emancipate from all manner of servitude.

CHAPTER TWO

FOR ETERNITY

With schooldays—as she thought—behind her, Mary Todd, during the summer of 1837, accepted an invitation to visit her relatives in Illinois. Her sister Frances had joined Elizabeth Edwards in Springfield the previous year. Mary planned to enter society in that promising community and, if she were lucky, find a husband.

There are several descriptions of Mary Todd at this time. Her eyes were said to be large and wide-set, deep blue and clear, and penetrating. Her upper lip was thin and somewhat prim; the lower one full and sensual. Although she was not considered beautiful, contemporaries called her "lovely." She was said to possess the most exquisite arms and shoulders in Lexington, with no bones or hollows showing. Her ready wit at times could be devastating.

The Springfield that was Mary Todd's destination had been little more than a crude, if ambitious, prairie village when her brother-in-law, Ninian W. Edwards, went there in 1833. At that time there were some 300 inhabitants, primitive buildings, and no public improvements.

In Kentucky, Ninian's father, wealthy Ninian Edwards, Sr., had served as a Supreme Court judge before crossing the Ohio River to serve as Governor of the Illinois Territory. Springfield was to enter the lively contest for the state capital's location, doing so well in the first balloting that ambitious men and women moved to the village in readiness for what they gambled would be the outcome. Some of their descendants found places in Illinois history. The railroad further opened up the area when the East-West division of the Northern Cross Railroad was begun on the banks of the Illinois River in 1832. Ten years later it reached Springfield.

The Springfield that Mary first knew had unpaved streets that were chaotic in winter, a condition not unusual in those days. (Years later she found the streets of Washington full of potholes and mud during the bad months of the year.) A public water supply and sewage system were still only dreams. Churches and schools were few, while the Edwards' handsome house was a landmark simply because there was nothing to surpass it. Business was booming; the main talk was "politics," a subject close to Mary's heart.

Mary was warmly welcomed to Springfield. Not only were her sisters delighted to have somebody visit them from home, but so were their neighbors, many of whom had migrated from Kentucky. Mary's niece, Katherine Helm, says,

> Mary, full of life and animation, was a great toast among her kinspeople who met her with open arms and vied with each other in entertaining her. All of them wanted to hear Lexington news told in Mary's own spicy fashion. She, fresh, young, and enthusiastic, was an ardent Whig like themselves, and could tell them the latest gossip of all the politicians in Kentucky. She gave her own views with vigor on the subject of slavery. She said that her stepmother agreed with her, indeed, that all the Humphreys believed, like Henry Clay, in the gradual emancipation of the slaves, and the preservation of the Union by compromises on its extension. She was interesting to old and young alike. To the older ones she showed a mature, cultivated mind, and among the younger and more frivolous ones her beautiful clothes and graceful dancing made her an object of interest and pride.

This reference to her stepmother is worth noting, for there had been disturbing signs that Betsy and her stepchildren were on unpleasant terms. Elizabeth Todd had not chosen to be married in her father's home, while Frances had left Kentucky as soon as she was old enough.

During that first visit Mary heard much of a certain young

lawyer who himself was a newcomer to Springfield, although she did not meet him. His name was Abraham Lincoln and he came from New Salem, a village located on the banks of the Sangamon River. Almost penniless, he had recently been admitted to the bar. He was said to like women yet in their presence to be exceedingly shy; he was scrupulously honest, a dangerous adversary in debate, and although his rugged, gaunt face could not be termed handsome, when softened by a smile it was the epitome of kindliness. His fame as a storyteller had not gone unnoticed; neither were the fits of melancholy and depression with which he was afflicted. A lonely man and a poor one, perhaps Mary's sisters did not choose to have him meet their sister. By their standards he was not much of a prize.

Among Mary's other Illinois relatives were her uncle, Dr. John Todd, and three lawyer cousins, John T. Stuart, Stephen T. Logan, and John J. Hardin. Both Hardin and Stuart had served with Lincoln in the Black Hawk War.

So Abraham Lincoln and Mary Todd, though practically neighbors, did not meet. Furthermore, in the late autumn of 1837, Mary Todd decided to return home in order to further her education.

That same fall Mary again enrolled in Dr. Ward's Spartan school for extra studies similar to the present-day postgraduate course. Her father and stepmother offered no objection, although a woman completing thirteen years of formal education was then something of a rarity. Few men ever received as much.

Because Betsy Todd was always sickly and tired, it is little wonder that there were clashes of temperament with her strong-willed and temperamental stepdaughter. Grandmother Parker, surrounded by her faithful servants, still lived too close to the Todd house, and Mary was her constant visitor. Neither she nor her old servants had ever forgiven Robert Todd for taking another wife.

A summer season of gaiety and parties helped pass Mary's last days in Lexington. Elizabeth Edwards sums up the situation in the Todd home when she says, "We had a vacancy in our family—wrote to Mary to come and make our home her home; she had a stepmother with whom she did not agree."

Frances Todd, their sister, had just married William Wallace, a doctor and druggist in Springfield. Neither father nor stepmother had attended the wedding.

It was cool, and the leaves were already beginning to change color on the trees when Nelson drove Mary in the family carriage to the Lexington and Ohio Railroad depot at Mill and Water Streets. The small steam locomotive called The Nottaway boasted a solitary coach built to hold twelve passengers inside and twelve on top. With the sharp toot of a whistle, Mary Todd's return journey to Springfield began. Feeling herself to be well-qualified to meet whatever life had to offer, she gazed back over the brown hemp fields toward the city of her childhood. The little train carried her to Frankfort, from where she traveled down river to Cairo. She then sailed up the Mississippi to St. Louis, and from there took a stage to Springfield.

It was good to be back! Lovingly she fingered the elegant white marble mantel in her sister Elizabeth's parlor. Here there was such a feeling of security; from that moment Springfield would be her true home.

This time she did not have to wait long before meeting Abraham Lincoln, almost ten years her senior, and the man about whom all Springfield was talking. Elizabeth Edwards might write somewhat cattily, "Lincoln could not hold a lengthy conversation with a lady; was not sufficiently educated and intelligent in the female line to do so," yet the fact remained that the up-and-coming lawyer-politician was dressing better, was welcome in the best homes, and was learning the kind of manners then required in polite society.

After two years of living in Springfield, Lincoln was now the law partner of Mary's cousin, Judge Stephen T. Logan, a leader of the Springfield bar. The law firm of Logan and Lincoln was well served by both partners, the latter having been invited to make the partnership with Logan because of his prowess as a trial lawyer. Logan was particularly good at seeing they were paid for their services—a blessing, for Lincoln was quite indifferent to making money. Instead, his great love was politics, to which the field of law was only a convenient stepping-stone. Having served four terms in the Illinois legislature, he was now seeking to better himself in political circles.

Lincoln first met Mary Todd at a cotillion which she attended, properly chaperoned by her sister, Mrs. Edwards. Mary, who loved to dance, was thoroughly enjoying herself, yet each time she circled the room with a new partner her eyes met those of "a tall, spare, but powerfully built man," in earnest conversation with her brother-in-law. Says Katherine Helm, "His face was a fascinating combination of poetic mysticism, earnest purpose, and a quaint humor. Just the kind of strength and ruggedness, too, that had attracted Mary when as a little girl she [Mary] had declared 'Henry Clay is the handsomest man in the town.'"

In this setting of candlelight and soft music, Abraham Lincoln and Mary Todd exchanged their first few words together. He quickly made an appointment to call upon her the next evening and "from that time they were on all occasions drawn irresistibly together."

What amazed Lincoln most was this young woman's apt knowledge of contemporary politics, particularly her first-hand information concerning slavery. Not only was she a born politician, but she had been raised in a home where politics were freely discussed. In addition, she had met and talked with all the chief Whigs in Kentucky, her family's home being one of their favorite meeting places. She even knew Henry Clay, whom Lincoln had once called his "beau-ideal of a statesman."

Now at last Mary Todd had somebody to listen to her own impassioned views on the plight of the American Negro—someone who shared her horror of the whipping post in the jail that stood within hearing of her Grandmother Parker's home. She was drawn to this tall, ungainly man who had declared in the legislature at Vandalia that "slavery is founded on both injustice and bad policy."

So there were meetings and more meetings, while all the time Mrs. Edwards fretted. To her sister, Frances, and other Springfield relatives she aired the opinion that Mary was making a grave mistake in preferring Lincoln to other more attractive Springfield men. Both sisters then reminded Mary of the dangers of such a union, that Lincoln's family were not their equals socially, nor did his education begin to match her own. What was even worse in their opinion, "he was ignorant of social forms and customs, he was indifferent to social position."

Such arguments failed with such a determined young woman as Mary Todd. Where Lincoln was concerned she was stubbornness itself, passionately defending him against the slightest criticism. Her favorite method of defense was to insist that one day Abraham Lincoln would become President of the United States. Some of her friends, upon hearing this, actually declared her mad, yet there is evidence that she made the remark to more than one reliable person who remembered and recorded it. One of them was a certain W. H. Lamon who recalled the earnest way in which she made the prophesy, never wavering in her belief.

Mary and Abraham were much in love in 1840. Engaged and planning to marry, the inexplicable happened. There was a sudden estrangement, more it would seem upon Lincoln's part than his intended bride's. Legend has embroidered the story with an arranged wedding that never was; a waiting bride and an embarrassed preacher. Frances Wallace, Mary's sister, is emphatic in denying this. "No," she declares, "it was as I tell you. There never was but one wedding arranged between Mary and Mr. Lincoln, and that was the time they were married."

Lincoln, at the last minute, became doubtful as to his ability to provide a wife with all the amenities she had up to that time enjoyed; he even doubted that he could make any woman happy. He went so far as to write Mary a letter which is thought to be essentially the same in content as one that he had written to Mary Owens, another girl in whom he had once been interested. He even read it aloud to his good friend, Joshua F. Speed, who immediately advised him to destroy it, which he did. Later, however, with his characteristic honesty, Lincoln told Mary of its contents. She cried a little but overlooked the incident. When the subject again troubled Lincoln, they actually parted yet Mary did not forget him. Writing a friend some months later, she still insisted that he would become President and given time, she hoped he would return to her.

Three weeks after the breaking of the engagement, Lincoln revealed his unhappiness when he wrote John T. Stuart of the "deplorable state" of his mind. "I am now the most miserable man living," he confided. "If what I feel were equally distributed to the whole human family, there would not be one cheerful face on the earth." What was more he was listless and ill, visiting Joshua F. Speed's farm home near Louisville. Finally, when the period of melancholy passed, he returned to Springfield, where Mary had not, as her sisters and other relatives so fondly hoped, fallen in love with somebody else.

A Mrs. Simeon Francis, whose husband, editor of Springfield's Whig newspaper, thought highly of Lincoln, in the role of matchmaker saw fit to bring the estranged lovers together in the privacy of her parlor. There she left them with the advice, "Be friends again." After that there were other secret meetings about which sister Elizabeth knew nothing, although later she was forced to admit that the enterprising Mrs. Francis had "shrewdly got them together." Once more Mary Todd and Abraham Lincoln fell in love—that is, if they had ever fallen out of it.

The time for advice, well-meaning or otherwise, was over for Mary Todd, who would take no further criticism of Abraham. His frankness and candidness, which so displeased her relatives, found only admiration in her eyes. They did not wish for a big wedding and so decided to be married quietly in the home of the Reverend Charles Dresser, the Episcopal minister.

All might have gone quietly, according to plan, if Lincoln had not by chance met Ninian Edwards, Mary's brother-in-law, on the street. With his usual frankness Lincoln informed Edwards that the marriage plans were set for that very evening. Edwards was more than surprised, declaring that, as he considered himself to be Mary's guardian, any wedding should be performed under his roof. Mary was then asked if she agreed and, after some brisk discussion on both sides, she did. Then hurrying to the home of her uncle, Dr. John Todd, of whom she was very fond, she blurted out, "Uncle, you must go and tell my sister that Mr. Lincoln and I are to be married this evening." Then she turned to her cousin, Elizabeth Todd, begging her to go on a last-minute shopping expedition.

Later at the Edwards' home, there was the other Elizabeth to contend with. She was most indignant that there was no time now for formal invitations. Dr. Todd soothed her, and Elizabeth Edwards rose to the spirit of the occasion. "It is fortunate, Mary," she said, "that you selected this evening, for the Episcopal sewing society meets with me and my supper is already ordered." Elizabeth Todd recalled that "this comfortable little arrangement did not suit Mary," who sent Uncle John off to inform Lincoln that there would be no wedding until next evening.

When it did take place on Friday, November 4, 1842, it was in the presence of some thirty relatives and friends. Entertainment followed the simple ceremony which, according to a contemporary, "was simple but in beautiful taste." The bride was radiant in one of her exquisitely embroidered white muslin gowns. Julia Jaye, Mary's confidante, who had known of her secret meetings with Abraham at the Francis home, and Elizabeth Todd were the bridesmaids, and Rodney Todd the attendant.

One amusing incident occurred during the ceremony, causing even the minister to laugh, for among the guests was the rough and jolly frontier Justice Brown of the Supreme Court, appropriately known as "The Falstaff of the Bench." This gentleman had never before seen such a formal wedding, with the minister in his robes of office reading the impressive Episcopal *Solemnization of Matrimony* from a Prayer Book. When the Reverend Dresser asked Abraham to repeat the words ". . . with all my worldly goods, I thee endow," the judge interrupted, "Lord Jesus Christ, God Almighty, Lincoln, the Statute fixes all that!"

Rain poured down, beating on the window-panes, while a high wind rattled at the doors. However, Mrs. Abraham Lincoln was too happy to think of the storm outside as she gazed lovingly at the simple gold wedding band that Abraham had given her, inscribed inside with the beautiful words: Love is Eternal.

CHAPTER THREE

MARRIED LIFE

They began their married life at the Globe Tavern where for the sum of four dollars a week they boarded with the Widow Beck. It was a far cry from the luxury Mary had known in her father's home at Lexington or even in her sister Elizabeth's fashionable house at Springfield. Even those members of the family who had disapproved of her choice of Lincoln as a husband now grudgingly admitted that she seemed very happy. Lincoln appeared to have lost much of the deep gloom which plagued him at intervals all of his life.

From the beginning Mary was determined to help Abraham prepare for what she prayed would be a successful political future. A seat in Congress would be a first major step. Gently she helped him to polish his manners and to attain a sense of ease when meeting people for the first time. He was careless about his clothes, so on cold days she made sure he was warmly clad. Boarding at the tavern, it was difficult to insure that he had all the nutritious foods she felt were essential to the welfare of his long lean frame and she dreamed of the day when they might have a home of their own. Financially these were to be Lincoln's lean years, of which John G. Nicolay writes, "He was so poor that he and his bride could not make the contemplated visit to Kentucky they would both have so much enjoyed."

Mary soon found that Abraham was a thrifty man, for in addition to supporting a bride he was helping his family and paying off some New Salem debts. There was little entertainment. Mary would mark pieces in the newspapers that she thought her husband should read. Sometimes of a wintry evening she even read them aloud to him. Red letter days were rare. When the circus came to town they went; there were concerts, and the jolly times when the strolling players visited Springfield.

Young Joseph Jefferson, the child actor, and his father, another Joseph, were in the theatrical company that the newlyweds enjoyed watching so much. Indeed, it was due to Lincoln's efforts that they were allowed to perform at all, for a narrow segment of Springfield's population considered acting to be an "unholy calling." Such pressures did these people put upon those in authority that a heavy license fee was levied upon the strolling players. With all available funds invested in the success of their show, the company were at a loss to know what to do. Then the managers heard of Lincoln and promptly engaged his legal services. Writes young Joseph in his autobiography,

> He had heard of the injustice, and offered, if they would place the matter in his hands, to have the license taken off, declaring that he only desired to see fair play, and he would accept no fee whether he failed or succeeded. The case was brought up before the council. The young lawyer began his harangue. He handled the subject with tact, skill, and humor, tracing the history of the drama from the time when Thespis acted in a cart to the stage of today. He illustrated his speech with a number of anecdotes, and kept the council in a roar of laughter; his good-humor prevailed and the exorbitant tax was taken off.

Young Joseph, whose most famous role was Rip Van Winkle, later found fame in theaters around the world.

Mary's sisters occasionally asked the players to their homes for dinner, and they were welcome guests at Uncle John Todd's. Most of socially-minded Springfield chose to ignore them.

On August 1, 1843, the Lincolns' first child, named Robert Todd for Mary's father, was born. Mary made all the baby clothes herself with the exception of those contributed as gifts by her sisters. Grandfather Todd even made a trip to Springfield to see young Robert, greeting him with an enthusiastic, "May God bless and protect my little namesake."

Robert Todd, during his visit to Springfield in 1843, seems to have been much impressed by his son-in-law. He assigned him several claims against Illinois merchants for unpaid cotton goods purchased from his Lexington factory. To Mary he gave eighty acres of land near Springfield. Best of all, he promised to make the Lincolns cash advancements of one hundred and twenty dollars a year until Lincoln's law practice was well established.

A nurse would have been an unnecessary expense, for Mary had known enough baby brothers and sisters to care adequately for an infant. Little Robert prospered under his mother's excellent attention. She enjoyed her baby, just as she enjoyed caring for Abraham. Marriage and motherhood fully occupied these early Springfield days and her life seemed complete when Abraham proudly announced that they would soon be able to purchase a house of their own. The gossips might call their first house "shabby," and maybe it was by the standards of her sisters and their friends. But these early days with Abraham and the new baby were the happiest and most contented she would ever know.

Shortly after Robert's birth, the Lincolns moved to a rented house on Fourth Street. Their stay was brief, for on May 1, 1844, they moved into what today, in its enlarged form—Mary having added an additional floor—is called the "Lincoln House." They had purchased this house for the sum of $1200 the previous January 16. Here Mary, or Puss, as Abraham affectionately called her, did her own housework. She made her dresses and even some of Abraham's clothes. As an experiment she cut out and pieced together a pair of large black velvet carpet slippers, gaily embroidering them with his initials.

Later there would be one servant to help, but not at first. Chaney, the cook in Lexington, would have been shocked could she have seen "Miss Mary" preparing meals in the kitchen. However, Mary Todd Lincoln had such willpower that she could master anything, and in a surprisingly short time she had become a tolerably good cook. Her table, though simply laid, was always adequate. She made sure the damask cloth was snowy white and, in

The Lincoln House, Springfield, Illinois. *Courtesy of the Illinois State Historical Society.*

season, that there were fresh flowers as a centerpiece. Abraham often remarked on the prettiness of their breakfast table; it made a happy beginning for a hard day. What silver she possessed was good and pleasing to the eye, yet a contrast to Betsy's massive silver in Kentucky.

Saving to better themselves, and with no help in the kitchen, Mary could not entertain like her sisters Elizabeth and Frances— and to be entertained, one has to reciprocate. Even a little later when they had their own cows, which Lincoln milked, they had few guests, as it was hard for a young wife and mother to compete with those other hostesses who had hired help.

As in all small communities, there was gossip, and it was whispered that Mary kept a sparse table so that what she saved on food could go toward buying new dresses. Bills from Smith's store show no such extravagances. Mrs. Lincoln was still making her own clothes, copying styles from pictures. She was more than a match for gossips during this stage of her life. Her tongue could be as sharp as theirs, and she gave them some tart answers. By thriftily saving, slowly she managed to purchase a rug or an item of furniture. Together she and Abraham would critically examine the latest acquisition, an event that always seemed to please Abraham, who never interfered in the household affairs. These he considered to be his wife's absolute domain.

Lincoln as an executive committee member of Springfield's Clay Club had a few weeks before their marriage invited Mary's childhood idol to visit Illinois.

At home in Lexington, where the painful question of slavery was reaching agitation point, Henry Clay, together with Mary's father and other friends, was publishing in pamphlet form the speeches of slavery's champion opponent, Robert J. Breckinridge. Such happenings were of vital interest to the Lincolns in Springfield, as indeed were all of Clay's doings.

Breckinridge's great adversary was Robert Wickliffe whose son, Robert Wickliffe, Jr., was running for Congress against Garret Davis. Davis had the support of Henry Clay, Robert S. Todd, and Clay's cousin, Cassius Marcellus Clay. The last-named had come under abolitionist influence while attending Yale and, after having heard a speech by William Lloyd Garrison, the journalist-abolitionist, had freed his own slaves. "Cash" Clay, as he was familiarly known, and Robert Wickliffe, Jr., had gone so far as to fight a duel, and although neither received a wound, slavery supporters in Lexington engaged the services of Samuel M. Brown of New Orleans, who was said to have had "forty fights and never lost a battle."

The day after he arrived the fiery Cash took exception to a statement made by young Wickliffe at a barbecue meeting held near Russell's Cave. At the sudden interruption, Brown knocked Cash down with a large cane. Getting to his feet, Cash took out his bowie knife and advanced upon Brown, who stood his ground with a pistol. Taking deliberate aim, when Cash was an arm's length away, the New Orleans strongman fired at his heart. While onlookers froze into horrified silence, Cash, apparently unharmed, opened up his assailant's head, cut off an ear, and demolished an eye! He then threw him into the cavern spring. Later it was found that the silver-lined scabbard of Cash's bowie knife had saved his life when the bullet struck. All there was to show was a red spot above his heart!

The outcome of this bloody affair, which the Lincolns followed in the press, was Cash Clay's charge of assaulting Samuel Brown with "intent to kill." His cousin Henry Clay acted as lawyer for the defense, assisted by John Speed Smith, uncle of Joshua Speed, Lincoln's friend. Much to everyone's surprise, Henry Clay won Cash an acquittal, which might be called the first victory of Lexington's anti-slavery faction. The delighted Lincolns read the result in Lexington's *Observer*.

For the next few years Lincoln's political career experienced its ups and downs. In 1843 he was defeated for Congress, following which he complained to an old friend, M. M. Morris of Menard County, that he had been rejected by Sangamon County because they had classed him as an aristocrat. Only Menard, the section of old Sangamon in which New Salem is now located, had given him their loyal support.

In 1844, Lincoln supported Henry Clay in his bid for the presidency, with dire results. Clay was defeated by James Knox Polk who, together with his hard-working wife, dark-haired Sarah Childress Polk, would prove a formidable husband-and-wife team in the

White House. Lincoln running as an elector for Henry Clay was himself defeated. It was a doubly bitter blow to Mary, seeing Clay and Abraham both go down in defeat. There was little consolation in reading afterward that President Polk's Inauguration Day was so wet that he seemed to be delivering his address to "a large assemblage of umbrellas."

There was consolation however in knowing that her husband's law practice flourished, and ironically, even through defeat his political influence increased. By 1847 he had defeated the famed backwoods preacher, Peter Cartwright, in a Congressional contest, and sat in the House of Representatives during the Mexican War. Although he opposed the hostilities, since he regarded the place where they had begun as outside American jurisdiction, he voted in favor of necessary army appropriations. Lincoln's attitude on propositions involving slavery indicated policies he was to follow thereafter: he voted for the Wilmot Proviso, which was a proposed amendment to a Congressional appropriations bill for the negotiation of peace with Mexico, and he wished to abolish slavery in the District of Columbia. The process for such abolition, he thought, should be gradual, undertaken with the local citizens' consent.

On March 10 of the previous year Mary had given birth to another son, whom they named Edward Baker after a friendly Congressman. With her sister Elizabeth undisputed leader of Springfield society, it would not have been natural had Mary not envied her a little. Abraham however had finally been elected to Congress, so that things would be different. Mary was also feeling somewhat homesick for Kentucky.

> Mother, dear, [she had written Betsy] I have been dreaming of our sweet old garden. I want to see it again, and even if, at this time of the year, it should be under its blanket of snow, I could still, in my mind's eye, see Elizabeth [Humphreys] strolling with me on the garden walk to the summer house.

Then, too, she naturally wanted to show off her sons. It was time to go home, so Lincoln decided to take her to Lexington before taking up their new winter abode in Washington. The happy event was duly recorded in Springfield's *Illinois Weekly* for October 28, 1847, as follows,

> Mr. Lincoln, the member of Congress elect from this district has just set out on his way to the city of Washington. His family is with him; they intend to visit their friends and relatives in Kentucky before they take up the line of march for the seat of government. Success to our talented member of Congress! He will find many men in Congress who possess twice the good looks, and not half the good sense, of our own representative.

On October 25, 1847, taking the stagecoach to St. Louis, the newly elected Representative to Congress for the Seventh District of Illinois, with his little family, boarded a steamboat bound for Louisville. On both the Indiana and the Kentucky banks were memories for Abraham, a blaze of autumn color. They passed Thompson's Landing where Lincoln's father, Thomas, and his family first crossed over the Ohio journeying from Rolling Fork to a new home in the Indian wilds. It seemed to Mary on that memorable trip that Abraham had an anecdote for every bend in the river.

In Louisville they took a train east to the Kentucky Bluegrass country. Mary could hardly control her excitement and it made Abraham happy to see such a childlike delight. They traveled the last part of the journey to Lexington by train on which, unknown to either party, Betsy's nephew Joseph Humphreys was a fellow passenger. The children were a handful and quite uninhibited, for neither parent felt able to treat them severely. The long-suffering Humphreys, the tranquility of his journey broken, was only too grateful to reach Lexington. He managed to reach the Todd home before the Lincolns.

"Aunt Betsy," he complained upon entering the door, "I was never so glad to get off a train in my life. There were two lively youngsters on board who kept the whole train in a turmoil, and their long-legged father, instead of spanking the brats, looked pleased as Punch and aided and abetted the older one in mischief."

He had hardly blurted out his story when up drove the Todd carriage with the offending family.

"Good Lord," cried young Humphreys, "there they are now!" Disappearing, he was not again in evidence during the Lincolns' visit.

It was a happy homecoming that November 3, and the style in which Mary had once lived, was quite a revelation to Lincoln. The house servants had lined themselves up behind the family in the front hall for it was a cold day. There were mingled cries of delight from everyone as Mary came in first carrying little Edward, or "Eddie" as they called him, in her arms.

Young Emilie, her half-sister recalls, "To my mind she was lovely; clear, sparkling, blue eyes, lovely smooth white skin with a fresh, faint wild-rose color in her cheeks; and glossy light brown hair, which fell in soft, short curls behind each ear. She was then about twenty-nine years of age."

Lincoln, wearing a close-fitting cap and ear muffs, strode into the hall behind his wife, a towering figure with little Robert in his arms. Emilie was so surprised at his height that she immediately thought of Jack and the Beanstalk, fearing that he might be the hungry giant of the fairy tale.

> He was so tall and looked so big with a long full black cloak over his shoulders and he wore a fur cap with ear straps which allowed but little of his face to be seen. Expecting to hear the "Fee, fi, fo, fum!" I shrank closer to my mother and tried to hide behind her voluminous skirts.

Lincoln probably sensed the child's uneasiness, for after shaking hands with the grownups, he stood Robert on the ground and swung the little girl up into his arms, saying in a tender voice, "So this is little sister." The child's fear immediately disappeared and from that day forward, Emilie Todd was always addressed as "Little Sister" by Mary's husband.

Sam Todd, who was in college at Danville, Kentucky, at the time, came home especially to see his sister and her family. He was so proud when Robert was taught to call him "Uncle." "What a big handsome boy Sam has grown to be. He was such a little scrap of a baby," teased Mary, to which remark Sam snapped, "Well, I at least have had the grace to grow up and you are still only a tiny little scrap hardly reaching to my shoulder." As an afterthought he added, "I hope my nephews will inherit their father's long legs." "And their mother's lovely disposition," said Mary rather tartly.

Emilie in particular remembered that pleasant visit all through her life. She enjoyed playing with Robert, "Bob" as they called him, noticing that Lincoln never seemed to be disturbed by all the noise they made. So absorbed was he in his books and newspapers that nothing seemed to distract him. Later she was told that his favorite reading was the *Niles Weekly Register*, a publication edited by H. Niles of Baltimore and Philadelphia containing "political, historical, geographical, scientific, astronomical, statistical and biographical documents, essays and facts." Lincoln also enjoyed the poetry dealing with the subject of slavery written by the English poet William Cowper. He bracketed the following timely lines:

> But Ah! What wish can prosper, or what prayer
> For merchants rich in cargoes of despair,
> Who drive a loathsome traffic, gauge and span,
> And buy the muscles and the bones of man?
> The tender ties of father, husband, friend,
> All bonds of nature in that moment end;
> And each endures, while yet he draws his breath,
> A stroke as fatal as the scythe of death.

She watched the Lincolns reading aloud together, listening somewhat in awe while her brother-in-law learned by heart William Cullen Bryant's melancholy verse, "Thanatopsis." Lincoln seemed prematurely obsessed by the subject of death, and Bryant's work, inspired by the English "Graveyard School" of poetry, was much to his liking. This particular poem sought comfort in nature for death. The earth, tomb of mankind, it reasoned, would cover all who presently laughed or chased their "favorite phantoms." Bryant advised that when one's own time came to join the "innumerable caravan"

> . . . . approach thy grave,
> Like one who wraps the drapery of his couch
> About him, and lies down to pleasant dreams.

Emilie noticed, too, how kind and courteous Mary was to the old slaves who, with many chuckles, reminded her of all her childhood pranks. Old Chaney was inveigled into giving Mary her verbal recipe for cornbread. Mary, businesslike, with notebook and pencil, soon became quite exasperated by Chaney's vague directions of "Jes' a pinch—jes' a leetle bit—sweeten to tas'."

Mary, with time to herself—for Sally, the old nurse, had already commandeered the baby Eddie—spent much time with her Grandmother Parker, who still lived in the same old brick house on Short Street, next to the house where Mary had been born. Lincoln was quick to note how devoted to the Widow Parker were her three old house slaves, Cyrus, Prudence, and Ann, upon whose services she was now, in her old age, totally dependent. Although such devotion was evident between master and house slave in many of the old homes that they visited, there was that other, more terrible aspect of slavery.

Only a few yards from the Widow Parker's side porch stood the infamous slave jail operated by W. A. Pullum, a dealer in human flesh. The front of Pullum's jail was located on Broadway, with living quarters for his own family upstairs. Downstairs there was a large double room complete with bar, where on wintry days prospective buyers could view Negroes who were for sale. At the rear of the building were rows of pens only eight feet square and seven feet high, with studded iron doors and little barred windows near the roof. The damp brick floors were covered with vermin-infested straw.

Lincoln had only to stand upon the Widow Parker's terrace for a clear view of the jail yard with all its degradation. He could not fail to heal the cries of the afflicted, chained to the whipping post. Within walking distance at the corner of Short and Mulberry Streets was another such jail where Negroes awaiting execution were incarcerated. Every few days there were slave auctions either at Cheapside, Lexington's most popular meeting place, or from the block in the courthouse yard.

Henry Clay was in residence at Ashland during the Lincolns' entire stay in Lexington. It was a happy experience when Mary took Abraham to meet "the sage of Ashland," whom he so much admired, and to whom she had been devoted since childhood. Clay was to give the Lincolns a large polished mahogany chest containing a set of cutlery on which a bas-relief of himself was delicately engraved into each ivory handle. It is today the property of Robert Lincoln Beckwith, Abraham's and Mary's great-grandson.

Clay's son, Henry Clay, had just been killed in the Mexican War, so that for Mary the visit was tinged with sorrow. The father bore his bereavement well, and on November 13 at the Courthouse, delivered a speech on the conduct of the war. The subject of slavery was introduced, giving Lincoln much food for thought. Said Clay,

> My opinions on the subject of slavery are well known. They have the merit, if it be one, of consistency, uniformity and long duration. I have ever regarded slavery as a great evil, a wrong, for the present I fear, an irremedial wrong to its unfortunate victims. I should rejoice if not a single slave breathed the air or was within the limits of our country. Among the resolutions which it is my intent to present for your consideration at the conclusion of the address one proposes in your behalf and mine, to disavow, in the most positive manner, any desire on our part to acquire any foreign territory whatever for the purpose of introducing slavery into it.

All too quickly the November days passed for Mary. Lexington was preparing a great welcome for their "hero," none other than Cassius Marcellus Clay, who had enlisted at once when the United States had declared war against Mexico. He had paused in his anti-slavery fight in his search for adventure. Five of his men had recently testified to Captain Clay's personal bravery when, after their capture, an order had been made for immediate execution.

Clay, facing the pistol of a Mexican major, cried out, "Kill me—kill the officers, but spare the men!" His words were in part heeded, and the men were marched barefoot and ragged to Mexico City. Clay insisted that they each take a turn at riding his mule.

Robert S. Todd had been chosen to deliver the welcome-home address. Ironically, Colonel Jesse Bayles, former member of the Committee of Sixty who had once invaded the editorial office of *The True American*, Clay's own publication, to berate him as a "nigger agitator" had now been chosen Grand Marshal for the ceremony.

Unfortunately the Lincolns could not stay in Lexington for the ceremony, for Abraham was due in Washington for the opening of Congress. On Thanksgiving Day he attended the old Presbyterian Church with Mary to hear Dr. Robert J. Breckinridge, famed orator and social crusader, give the sermon. That same afternoon, there were tearful farewells, especially for Emilie, when the Lincolns boarded the stage headed for Maysville. From there they took the steamboat up the Ohio River en route to Washington.

A new era had begun for all of them.

WASHINGTON AT LAST

It was late on the evening of December 2, 1847, when the Lincoln family arrived by train in the capital. The boys were tired and irritable, which was hard on their mother, who was suffering from one of the sick headaches that troubled her. Washington's railroad station was little more than a huge wooden shed located at Pennsylvania Avenue and Second Street. Here gangs of idle young toughs were always on hand to meet the two daily trains from Baltimore, the last stop before Washington. They were a poor advertisement for America's chief city, yet were really little worse than the horde of hackney-cab drivers who rushed up to unfortunate passengers, not asking but demanding their patronage.

The Lincolns had booked temporary accommodation at Brown's Hotel, an establishment much patronized by members of Congress, especially Southerners. In years to come Brown's Hotel would achieve a marble-fronted grandeur together with a new name, the Metropolitan. It was bitterly cold as they drove to the hotel. With her throbbing head, Mary was more aware of the frozen ruts in the uneven road than the others. Finally, settled in their warm rooms, Abraham helped undress the children for bed. As soon as her head touched the pillow Mary found relief. Next morning she was better. There was little peace until she had taken the boys for a drive. Abraham went about his business, for on December 6, the following Monday, the Thirtieth Congress of the United States was due to convene.

Washington at Last : : *page 39*

Mary was immediately struck by the fact that Washington appeared so Southern. To be sure the romantic quaintness was missing, but there was that certain atmosphere of indolence, happy disorder, and lack of sanitation. Shanty and mansion stood in harmony, side by side. Southern-planter members of Congress were easily identified around the hotel by their accents, wide brimmed hats, and frequent calls for mint juleps. Their body slaves stood chattering in clusters around the hotel door. Outside, the streets were filled with a babel of horse-drawn carriages, flocks of geese, squealing hogs, and an occasional cow, all mixed up with the foot travelers. It was a wonder, thought Mary, that there were not more accidents.

The livestock, she soon found out, were the city scavengers. Anyone who disturbed their unsavory task was liable to a fine. The boys were delighted with the wallowing pigs on Capitol Hill. Mary was less enthusiastic, for walking was hazardous when the inhabitants threw their slops right on to the streets and rough sidewalks. They dropped dead cats and dogs in the city canal. Washington was in urgent need of order and beautification.

Only two city streets were paved, and then only in part, while with one exception the meager sidewalks were poorly constructed of gravel and ashes. It was sheer torture, Mary discovered, to drive down Pennsylvania Avenue, the chief thoroughfare, for its huge cobblestones had been laid so unevenly. Only when the streets were covered with snow was a ride made bearable. Then horse-drawn sleighs were the means of transportation. On part of Pennsylvania Avenue there were smoking oil lamps which were lighted when Congress was in session.

Less than thirty thousand white people were living in Washington at the time of Mary's first visit. In addition there were eight thousand free Negroes and two thousand slaves for, to its shame, the city still boasted a good share of the domestic slave trade and had done so since 1802. The sight of more Negroes in chains reminded Mary of those hated scenes from her childhood. It seemed incredible that for almost fifty years slaves had passed by the very windows of the Capitol on their way to Southern servitude. Such dismal sights provided excellent propaganda material for abolitionists.

Mary often discussed the problem with Abraham, who called the District of Columbia's slave trade a "sort of Negro livery stable." Here droves of Negroes were collected, temporarily kept, and finally taken south to market. Fortunately it was wintertime, so that the keen air abated the stench from the night soil carts as they rolled slowly on their way to the Commons, only ten blocks north of the White House. Polluted well-water was often the cause of outbreaks of epidemics.

Even the public buildings seemed disorderly, for several were still unfinished. Neither wing of the Capitol was begun, while over the central portion still rose the wooden dome. Foundations for the Smithsonian Institution had just been laid. A foreign visitor likened the scene to "a frame of Berlin wool work in which the fair embroideress has made spasmodic attempts at a commencement." Anthony Trollope, the English novelist, was even less kind. "Tucking your trousers up to your knees," says he, "you will lose yourself among rude hillocks, you will be out of the reach of humanity. . . . If you are a sportsman, you will desire to shoot snipe within sight of the President's house."

Mary quickly discovered that most of the shops and stores were located on Pennsylvania Avenue but that they were poorly stocked and equipped. All the important shopping had to be done in Baltimore, then a two-and-a-half-hour journey by train.

A few days after their arrival, Abraham moved his family to a boarding house belonging to Mrs. Ann G. Spriggs, situated in Carroll Row, on Capitol Hill. This area was populated by quiet church-going people who, in warm weather, sat on their porches and doorsteps. Close by stood a few convenient shops including one, much in demand, where needles and ribbons could be bought. There was a taffy dealer who had the unsanitary habit of spitting in the palms of his hands when making brittle candy!

As few Congressional members brought their wives to Washington, there were few women residents in hotels or boarding houses. This was probably the reason why Mary seldom appeared in the public rooms at Mrs Spriggs', although she did come in for meals. However, Robert was particularly conspicuous to the other guests because he always seemed to have his own way. Abraham was the life of the dining room with his wealth of amusing stories and anecdotes, though his solitary recreation was bowling.

Mary had little time for socializing, for her days were fully taken up by her two boisterous boys. She enjoyed listening to stories of the Executive Mansion, even though Abraham's fellow Congressmen complained of the austere entertaining of President Polk and his "excellent" wife. They both believed that they had been "hired" by the country to work, and therefore banned dancing and refreshments in the White House.

The White House grounds were open to the public, although winter was not the right time to enjoy them. Mary longed for a glimpse of the aged Dolley Madison, that famed First Lady who had saved George Washington's portrait from burning in the War of 1812. At President Polk's White House Reception in February of 1849, Dolley, at eighty-two, wore a youthful low-cut gown. Her arms and shoulders were, commented an eyewitness, "remarkably beautiful." Mrs. Alexander Hamilton, "a tiny little woman" was also still active in Washington, though now very old.

While he was in Washington, Lincoln had entrusted his Springfield affairs to William Henry Herndon, who had accepted the invitation to become Lincoln's junior law partner in 1844. Billy, as Lincoln liked to call him, was a young man who was disliked by Mary as much as he disliked her. Years before, when she was still unmarried, Herndon had asked Mary to dance with him, after which he had blurted out, "I want to compliment you on the grace of your dancing. You glide through the waltz with the ease of a serpent." She had not been amused, icily replying, "Mr. Herndon, comparison to a serpent is rather severe irony." Mary had never liked Herndon since.

With much pride, Mary kissed her husband goodbye as he left for the first time to take his seat in Congress. She had seen that he was neatly dressed, and checked that he had a large handkerchief. "The lone Whig from Illinois," the newspapers had dubbed him. As she watched his tall, gangling figure amble leisurely out of the house, it was, she thought, a big step toward the White House.

Unfortunately the seat allotted him was one of the poorest, for

Number 191 was in the center back row of the section to the left of the Speaker. Just in front of him, and only four seats to the right, sat George Ashmun of Massachusetts, a man destined twelve years later to preside over the same National Republican Convention that would nominate Lincoln for the Presidency. Far to the right, but in the same row as Ashmun sat Joshua R. Giddings of Ohio, a bold and violent abolitionist.

One of the best House seats was occupied by its most illustrious member, former President John Quincy Adams, then in his eighty-second year. After leaving the White House, he had entered Congress, serving in nine successive Congresses. The former President collapsed in his seat from paralysis less than six weeks after Abraham entered the House.

Lincoln—to Mary's great satisfaction—was assigned to the Committee on Post Offices and Post Roads, and also to the Committee dealing with Expenditures in the War Department. They were both good appointments. On December 13 he had written to Herndon, "As you are all so anxious for me to distinguish myself, I have concluded to do so before long." On January 8, 1848, he was further able to inform his law partner that in making his first verbal report he was badly scared but no more than when he spoke in court at Springfield. Although few new Congressional members have been so active as Lincoln, unfortunately he made little impression and that was not favorable; his Illinois constituents had not expected him to oppose the Mexican War. He had been in the House hardly two weeks when he introduced critical resolutions questioning the validity of the war and the Administration's handling of it. With interest Mary noted that some of the Washington press correspondents had commented on her husband's stand. The Rockford (Illinois) *Forum* on January 19, 1848, quoted from the Baltimore *Patriot* that "evidently there is music in that very tall Mr. Lincoln." Unfortunately for Lincoln, the people of Illinois were annoyingly to remind him of that Mexican music for many years to come.

On the night of January 19, Henry Clay spoke before a great crowd in the hall of the House of Representatives. The occasion was the annual meeting of the American Colonization Society. Lincoln was present and later Mary made him repeat almost word for word what Clay had said. The highlight, and the spot where Clay drew the most applause, was when he told the story of a stranger from Alabama who had recently died, willing Clay his slaves. Clay had persuaded twenty-three of them to take up their lives in free Liberia, and they had recently sailed to their new homes from New Orleans.

During that cold Washington winter, life was rather restricted for Mary and her two little boys at the Widow Spriggs' boarding house. In the early spring, Abraham, feeling that his wife needed a change of scene, for her headaches were more frequent, sent her with the children back to Lexington. He was soon to regret the decision, for in a letter dated April 16 we find him complaining of his loneliness,

> In this troublesome world, we are never quite satisfied. When you are here, I thought you hindered me some in attending to business but now, having nothing but business —no vanity—it has grown exceedingly tasteless to me. I hate to sit down and direct accounts, and I hate to stay in the old room by myself. You know I told you in last Sunday's letter I was going to make a little speech during the week and the week has passed away without my getting a chance to do so and now my interest in the subject has passed away too. Your second and third letters have been received since I wrote before. Dear Eddy thinks father is gone tapets.

Mary had asked him to buy Eddie some plaid stockings, the latest rage for little boys. Prince Albert, Queen Victoria's husband, had popularized the Scottish plaid, so that dresses, shawls and even wallpapers were so designed, even in republican America!

> I went yesterday to hunt the little plaid stockings as you wished, but found that McKnight has quit business and Allen had not a single pair of the description you gave and only one plaid of any sort that I thought would fit "Eddy's

dear little feet." I have a notion to make another trial
tomorrow morning. If I could get them, I have an excellent
chance of sending them. Mr Warrick Tunstall, of St. Louis
is here. He is to leave early this week and to go by
Lexington. He says he knows you, and will call to see you,
and he voluntarily asked if I had not some package to
send to you.

Grandmother Parker's house had recently been broken into, and Abraham asked if there were any further developments in the distressing incident. A gold watch and some monogrammed silverware had been stolen. Promptly Mary's grandmother offered one hundred dollars as a reward for their recovery. "If I were she I would not remain there alone," he advised, for the old lady's faithful retainers were almost as aged as she. Then he writes of the boarding house, revealing that even in such cramped quarters and with two noisy youngsters whose presence at times must surely have been hard on the other boarders, his wife had made friends. "All the house or rather all with whom you were on decided good terms send their love to you. The others say nothing."

Abraham was delighted about her improved state of health; excited about a new purchase he had made; embarrassed because she addressed his letters with the prefix "Hon."; and once more spoke nostalgically about their children.

Very soon after you went away, I got what I think a very
pretty set of shirt bosom studs—modest little ones jet set in
gold only costing 50 cents a piece or 1.50 the whole.
    Suppose you do not prefix the "Hon." to the address
on your letters to me any more. I like the letters very much
but I would rather they should not have that upon them.
It is not necessary as I suppose you have thought to have
them come free.
    And you are entirely free from headache? That is good
—considering it is the first spring you have been free from
it since we were acquainted—I am afraid you will get so
well and fat and young as to be wanting to marry again.

Tell Louisa I want her to watch you a little for me. Get weighed and write me how much you weigh. I did not get rid of the impression of that foolish dream about dear Bobby, till I got your letter written the same day.

What did he and Eddie think of the little letters father sent them? Don't let the blessed fellows forget father.

He always sent Mary money, for although she was staying at her father's home and visiting much with her grandmother, he liked her to feel independent. He thought that after the first penurious years together she deserved some money of her own.

Mary replied in a long, gossipy letter, sharing every trivial detail of her daily life:

Lexington, May———, 48.

My Dear husband:

You will think indeed that old age has set its seal upon my humble self, that in few or no letters I can remember the day of the month. I must confess it is one of my peculiarities.

I feel wearied and tired enough to know that this is Saturday night, our babies are asleep, and as Aunt Maria B. is coming for me tomorrow morning, I think the chances will be rather dull that I should answer your last letter tomorrow.

I have just received a letter from Frances W., it related in especial manner to the box I had desired her to send, she thinks with you (as good persons generally agree) that it would cost more than it would come to, and it might be lost on the road. I rather expect she has examined the special articles and thinks, as Levi says, they are rather hard bargains. But it takes so many changes to do children, particularly in summer, that I thought it might save me a few stitches. I think I will write her a few lines this evening, directing her to send them. She says Willie is just recovering from another spell of sickness, Mary or none of them are well. Springfield, she reports, as dull as usual—Uncle S. was to leave there on yesterday for Ky.

Our little Eddie has recovered from his spell of sickness—Dear boy, I must tell you a little story about Him. Bobby in his wanderings today, came across in a yard a little kitten, your hobby; he says he asked a man for it. He brought it triumphantly to the house. So soon as Eddie spied it, his tenderness broke forth, he made them bring it water, fed it with bread himself with his own dear hands, he was a delighted little creature over it. In the midst of his happiness Ma came in. She, you must know, dislikes the whole race of cats. I thought in a very unfeeling manner, she ordered the servant near to throw it out which of course was done—Ed screaming and protesting loudly against the proceeding. She never appeared to mind his screams, which were long and loud, I assure you. 'Tis unusual for her nowadays to do anything quite so striking, she is very obliging and accommodating, but if she thought any of us were on her hands again, I believe she would be worse than ever. In the next moment she appeared in a good humor. I know she did not intend to offend me. By the way, she has just sent me up a glass of ice-cream, for which this warm evening I am duly grateful.

The country is so delightful I am going to spend two or three weeks out there, it will doubtless benefit the children. Grandma has just received a letter from Uncle James Parker of Miss. saying he and his family would be up by the twenty-fifth of June, would remain here some little time and go on to Philadelphia to take their oldest daughter there to school. I believe it would be a good chance to pack up and accompany them. You know I am so fond of sight-seeing and I did not get to New York or Boston, or travel the lake route. But, perhaps, dear husband, like the irresistible Col. Mc. cannot do without his wife next winter and must needs take her with him again, I expect you would cry aloud against it.

How much I wish, instead of writing, we were together this evening. I feel very sad away from you.

Ma and myself rode out to Mr Bell's splendid place this afternoon to return a call. The house and grounds are magnificent. Frances W. would have died over their rare exotics.

It is growing late, these summer eves are short, I expect my long scrawls for truly such they are, weary you greatly. If you come on in July or August, I will take you to the Springs. Patty Webb's school in S. closes the first of July. I expect Mr. Webb will come for her. I must go down about that time and carry on quite a flirtation (you know we always had a penchant that way).

I must bid you goodnight. Do not fear the children have forgotten you. I was only jesting. Even E's brighten at the mention of your name.
My love to all,
Truly yours
M.L.

The mention of the kitten related to the story that when Abraham had stayed with Nat Grigsby at Gentryville in 1844, a cat, vouched Nat, "began mewing, scratching, and making a fuss generally"; that Abraham who had retired for the night "got up, took the cat in his hands," and stroking its back "gently and kindly, made it sparkle."

The correspondence between husband and wife continued. On July 2 Abraham inquired about some purchases.

Last Wednesday, P. H. Hood & Co., dunned me for a little bill of $5.38 cents, and Walter Harper & Co., another for $8.50 cents, for goods which they say you bought. I hesitated to pay them, because my recollection is that you told me when you went away, there was nothing left unpaid. Mention in your next letter whether they are right.

"I have had no letter from home," he complains,

since I wrote you before, except short business letters, which have no interest for you.

By the way, you do not intend to do without a girl, because the one you had has left you? Get another as soon as you can to take charge of the dear codgers. Father expected to see you all sooner, but let it pass; stay as long as you please, and come when you please. Kiss and love the dear rascals.

Affectionately,
A. LINCOLN.

Abraham certainly did not begrudge Mary or his adored "codgers" a good time. For them the happiest day of their stay in Kentucky was that on which the circus came to town. At noon on a cloudless August day, Howe's Great Circus and Collection of World Curiosities, heralded by blaring bandsmen, paraded right past the Todd residence on Main Street. There at the same gate through which Mary and her cousin Elizabeth as youngsters had watched those tragic "parades" of shackled Negro slaves, young Eddie and Bob stood wide-eyed and excited. The procession was led by an exotic "Egyptian Dragon Chariot pulled by twelve trained Syrian camels." In the chariot sat what a contemporary report describes as the "Full New York Brass Band." Behind came Queen Mab's "Fairy Chariot" all glittering and white, drawn by twelve Shetland ponies driven by the "celebrated Dwarf, Major Stevens." Red-nosed clowns turned somersaults while a troop of "Real Bedouin Arabs" competed for attention with eight somewhat plump equestrian ladies. There were wild beasts reputedly from the far jungles of Africa, their sad, red-flecked eyes glaring menacingly from gilded cages.

An event of a different nature and one which Mary knew would interest Abraham occurred on Sunday morning, August 5, when seventy-five armed and desperate slaves escaped from their Fayette County masters to head for the Ohio River and sanctuary. The infuriated owners soon discovered that Patrick Doyle, a student at Center College, Danville, had masterminded the escape. Hundreds of Bluegrass men formed posses to apprehend the runaways and their leader, who a few days later were surrounded in the hempfields north of Cynthiana village. Doyle was carried in irons to the dreaded Megowan's jail where he was immediately placed in solitary confinement pending trial.

Thundered an editorial in the local *Observer,*

> It is time that a more severe example should be made of these wretches, and every citizen should be on the alert to detect and bring them to punishment. That there are abolitionists in our midst—emissaries from this piratical crew—whose business it is to tamper with and run off our slaves, there is not the shadow of doubt.

Mary read it with mixed feelings, for she shared the sentiments of the young Reverend William M. Pratt, pastor of Lexington's First Baptist Church, who wrote in his diary, "Some will be hung I fear, all the others will probably be sent down the river. They were a class of the finest negroes in the county."

Part of Mary's summer was spent visiting the Todds' summer home that stood on high ground near the Leestown Pike. It boasted the lovely name of Buena Vista.

A large frame house with tall sturdy brick chimneys, Buena Vista was sheltered by a group of feathery locust trees. There was a double portico in front, and a long porch connected two stone slave cabins to the main house. The views were magnificent; a little brook ran through the woods at the foot of the hill.

Lincoln had hoped to join his family when Congress adjourned, promising them a trip to Crab Orchard Springs. This proved impossible, for the Presidential campaign of General Zachary Taylor, familiarly dubbed "Old Rough-and-Ready," had hit a snag in New England. After Congress adjourned on August 14, Lincoln had to accompany General Leslie Combs of Lexington on a morale-boosting trip to the Massachusetts Whigs. Wearing a long linen "duster," Lincoln stumped from Worcester to Boston for the hero of the Mexican War. At Tremont Temple in Boston he shared the platform with William H. Seward, a man destined to play a supporting role in his future.

There were also difficulties at home for, according to Herndon's letters, the Whigs were in trouble in Sangamon County. Young men had never taken a lead in the party, prompting Lincoln to chide them in a letter to his partner, ". . . you must not wait to be brought forward by the older men. For instance, do you suppose that I should ever have got into notice if I had waited to be hunted up and pushed forward by older men."

Herndon was encouraged enough to form a "Rough-and-Ready Club" in Springfield, whose members were soon filling the streets with the Whig's rousing song.

> Come fall in, boys, eyes right and steady,
> And raise the shout for *Rough-and-Ready*,
> He licked old Peg-leg with his Pass
> And now he'll use Lewis Cass.

At the beginning of October, Mary and her sons left Lexington to join Abraham in Chicago en route for Springfield and the home they had not seen for almost a year. Abraham was delighted with the appearance of his suntanned boys, to say nothing of the healthy appearance of his wife. Kentucky had done her good; at last she seemed free of the troublesome headaches, calm, and at ease. It had been an easy summer, for Betsy had been uncommonly pleased to see her. There had been no real friction.

The Lincolns stayed for two days at the Sherman House, but even then their reunion was interrupted by politics. At six hours' notice Lincoln was asked to speak at the courthouse, but when he arrived there the large crowds necessitated the meeting's removal to the public square. For two hours Mary sat and listened to her husband pressing home his points. How well he had developed, she thought; the New England campaign had mellowed him and taught him how to use his humor more convincingly. It was the best address she could ever remember his giving, and next day, to her delight, she discovered that the Chicago *Daily Journal* agreed with her, calling it "one of the very best we have heard or read since the opening of the campaign."

Soon they were in their own home again, with Abraham helping the men bring down their furniture from the north bedroom. It was good to see him so happy; separation had only drawn them closer together.

Somewhat surprisingly, there had been no news of the

Interior of the Lincoln House, Springfield, Illinois. *Courtesy of the Illinois State Historical Society.*

Lincolns' homecoming in the local press. Ten days later, Lincoln set out to campaign for the Whigs in Petersburg, Jacksonville, Tremont, and Pekin. Nobody quite knew what Old Rough-and-Ready stood for, or what kind of President he would make. Even his own wife, Margaret, an aging invalid, argued that he had already done enough for the country, and should be allowed to spend his twilight years in peace.

The Whig campaign was being fought on the basis of David Wilmot's Proviso that no form of slavery could at any time be introduced into new territories acquired from Mexico. Mary was still uneasy that Abraham had damaged his political career in Illinois because of his unpopular local stand on the war. Even so she had to admit that as the lone Whig Congressman from Illinois he was drawing large crowds wherever he went.

In November, when Zachary Taylor was elected President of the United States, in Illinois, to Lincoln's chagrin, the Whigs were hopelessly defeated. Ironically the new Administration, for which he had campaigned so hard and faithfully, gave him no credit for its victory. Disillusioned and hurt he prepared to return to Washington to serve out the remaining months of his Congressional term.

This time Mary decided not to accompany him. His political future now seemed so uncertain that she deemed it prudent to stay in their own home, rather than give him the added expense of providing extra fares and accommodation for herself and the boys in Washington. Also she was disappointed that he did not think he might be in line for a Cabinet post. In fact, he appeared to be helping everybody but himself to attain important government positions. He had even promised to help Ninian Edwards' uncle, Cyrus Edwards, to obtain the post of Commissioner of the Land Office, a post that would have suited Abraham himself admirably.

A letter from Lincoln's father Thomas Lincoln, written by John D. Johnston, his step-brother, begging for twenty dollars at once, or "Father would lose his land," came at a time when Lincoln was worried over his own troubles. Mary had never liked her thriftless Lincoln in-laws, and she could only sympathize with her husband's predicament. The step-brother took pains to inform Lincoln that he too owed seventy or eighty dollars which, having neither cash nor property, he could not possibly repay. Promising that if his step-brother would send one hundred dollars he should have all the land "when Father dies" he pleaded,

> I am dund and doged to death So I am most tired of living and I would all most Swop my Place in *Heaven* for that much money. I know you will think little of this for your never had the Tryal, but Abe, I would drother Live on bread and wotter than to have men allways duning me.

Mary was relieved when Abraham responded "cheerfully" to his father's request for the twenty dollars to save his land, yet ignored the plea of the hapless John.

Lincoln returned to Congress still feeling that the people he had sought to serve honestly and well had not appreciated his services. The General Land Office appointment remained a bone of contention, for now it seemed that the only way it could be secured for Illinois was for Lincoln to seek it himself. However his loyalty to the Edwards family had caused him to wait too long, and the post went to Justin Butterfield.

Abraham returned to Mary sick and thwarted, and without having eaten for days. Although in the long run the discipline of defeat would be good for him, it still seemed an injustice, for the fortunate Butterfield had not even campaigned for President Taylor, as Lincoln had done. Now he had been given a fine political plum.

When it was suggested that Lincoln would make a good governor for the Oregon Territory, Mary was adamant that he refuse. To send him two thousand miles to serve in what was still little more than a wilderness would cut him off from the mainstream of the nation. She knew it would be political suicide. The "most ambitious woman I ever saw," as her sister Elizabeth Edwards once called her, was far from feeling defeated!

CHAPTER FIVE

A DEATH IN THE FAMILY

With Abraham back in his dingy law office, Mary set about making their home more comfortable, spending some of the savings she had kept in readiness for such an occasion. She was a very clean housekeeper, although she did not particularly enjoy housework. She kept two large pans of water, one hot for washing and the other cold for rinsing, upon the long kitchen table where Abraham and the boys could freshen up before meals. They never talked politics while eating. This was a family time which they shared with their boys.

Tirelessly she had tramped from one store to another getting provisions for her larder, buying in bulk, which was the custom of the times. Sacks of rice and flour, stone jars filled with tasty preserves, baskets packed with onions and potatoes. She traded in her old Empire stove for a brand new Buck model, bargaining in a way that would have pleased Chaney, the cook back in Kentucky. She used her deep iron kettle for making the family soap. Her spider frying pan hung on the chimney. At the back of the new stove were the carefully scrubbed waffle iron, presser iron, and the big roaster which was put to good use every Sunday and holiday.

Mary bathed in the large tin tub which Abraham would carry into the kitchen, placing it in front of the warm stove. He preferred to use the men's bathing room at the City Hotel, for he found that to cramp his long legs into the small tub was too uncomfortable. Mary would wrap his razor, soap, and comb inside a large towel. For herself it was pleasant to bathe in the hot kitchen, now smelling pleasantly of lavender-water.

Watching the boys at play, Mary spent her time diligently sewing red draperies of corded silk for the sitting room. These Abraham hung from high cornices. She then made brocatel draperies to hang in the parlor. It was useful having a tall husband for such domestic problems.

In the parlor she chose dark green paint, and for the sitting room a gay wallpaper flecked with little blue and white flowers. This latter room and the entrance hall were each livened with serviceable ingrained carpet.

They kept their big round table which Abraham had insisted upon buying her for their quarters at the Globe Tavern, although there were those of her more elegant relatives who thought it a monster. On it she neatly piled the newspapers and books which she thought Abraham should read. Her mending basket, which was continually in use, stood upon her most prized possession, a real French marble-topped table which held pride of place between the windows looking out over Eighth Street. She bought a new fold-top table which, should the occasion ever arise, could seat a fair-sized dinner party; a set of rung-back chairs with caned seats; a fashionable high sideboard to hold the candelabra and silver platters they had received as wedding gifts but seldom used. Finally, she purchased two comfortable high-backed Boston rockers to stand on either side of the sitting room fireplace, with smaller ones for Bob and Eddie.

In all these affairs of the home Abraham showed genuine interest, promising that when he managed to get some good, paying clients he would build her a white picket fence and a brick wall to insure some measure of privacy.

With Bob old enough to attend Mr. Estabrook's day school, something had to be done about his crossed eyes. The Lincolns' physician, Dr. Wallace, sent him to a Dr. Sandford Bell, a former surgeon at the New York Metropolitan Medical College. He was much in favor of an operation originated by a Dr. Dieffenbach in Germany to correct the situation.

Mary was as possessive of her children as she was of her husband. The drawings depicting the operation appalled her, particularly when she learned that should the corrective measure fail, the iris would go to the corner of the eye where it would remain permanently.

Abraham was as disturbed as she for they adored and spoiled their sons. He was too upset to accompany her upon the morning of the surgery, which Dr. Wallace had prevailed upon them to let Bob undergo. She had to sit in the room while the two doctors, Wallace and Bell, roped Bob into a high chair while he screamed with fright. So violent did he become that it was necessary to enlist another doctor to help steady the terrified child. White with horror she watched, hands gripping the side of her chair, while Dr. Bell used double hooks to part the reluctant eyelids, then swiftly cut the mucous membrane to expose the offending muscle. Nauseated, she lurched forward as the surgeon quickly snipped the muscle. The operation was over, a bandage was quickly fixed in place. Somehow Bob managed to run over and clutch her knees which were so weak that it was some minutes before she could trust herself to stand up without fear of fainting.

She was still nursing Bob at home when a black-edged envelope arrived from her stepmother with the news of Robert Todd's untimely death from cholera. It was a terrible shock to Mary, whose memories of her father were such happy ones. Perhaps she had been closer to him than her other sisters in Springfield, for their grief did not go as deeply as her own. Abraham was, as ever, kind and a good listener as she recalled such trivial incidents as the doll her father had brought from New Orleans when she was a child, or of how he had insisted she be educated as thoroughly as any boy.

Robert Todd had overtaxed his strength in his efforts to be re-elected to the Kentucky Senate at a time when feelings were running high over the slavery problem. When plague, in the form of cholera, had struck Lexington he had been in the midst of his campaign trips in all the outlying hamlets, canvassing for votes. He was grateful that Betsy and the children were enjoying the comparative safety of Buena Vista for the summer.

Meanwhile in Lexington the death carts rumbled through the

streets each night, collecting bodies to be buried. Yards of black crepe hung from the doorposts of stricken homes.

Todd and other candidates were obliged to make long horseback rides into the countryside in search of votes. Tired out, on July 9 he had spoken at Spencer's Mill near the village of Fort Springs. The following Tuesday he was taken with a chill. As he grew worse he made his will and signed it. On July 16, 1849, he died.

As the cemeteries had filled because of the pestilence, his body was buried beneath the ancient moss-covered oaks in Boswell's Woods on the top of a slope. Below was the spring beside which his father, together with other Kentucky hunters, had camped and named the town of Lexington.

Mary read two reports of her father's death, besides the facts contained in Betsy's letter. The Lexington *Observer & Reporter* on July 18 had called him "the noblest work of God—an honest man." The *Illinois Daily Journal* for July 28 erroneously described the cause of death as "brain fever," although when Mary later inquired as to what treatment had been given, she found that the standard remedy for cholera had been used: rhubarb, calomel, and opium.

As the days passed Mary heard of many Lexington acquaintances who had been quickly taken. Forty people had died in one day alone. Many stores closed down on Main Street; the rich fled north in search of safety; several of the doctors themselves succumbed. Cannon were fired on the advice of Transylvania scientists, who believed that this would rid the air of pestilence.

In spite of everything, the election campaign continued, and Lincoln followed its course in the *Observer*. To his and Mary's concern, every emancipation candidate was defeated. Brave, farseeing men whom he admired, like the great Henry Clay, had failed to solicit any real favor for the cause of gradual emancipation in the state of Kentucky.

Robert S. Todd had willed the greater part of his estate to Betsy, his second wife, with the slaves to be hers for life and then to go to her children. The rest of his property was to be "divided equally in just proportions" between his "first and second children." Unfortunately for Betsy, the will was only witnessed by one person, so that when it was presented for probate at the September term of the Fayette County Court, Mary's youngest brother, George Todd, challenged the validity of the document. His grounds were that it lacked the second witness as required by Kentucky law. George's objection was sustained and the estate was ordered to be shared equally among the various heirs.

Betsy still had six young children out of the eight she had borne Robert Todd, totally dependent upon her for support. Now she was forced to have all of his holdings converted into immediate cash, including his one-third interest in the firm of Oldham, Todd and Company. The proceeds then had to be divided among all of Robert's fourteen children.

When the news reached Springfield, Mary and her sisters decided that, as probate had been refused, even though they themselves had done nothing to prove the original will invalid, Abraham should go to Lexington as legal counsel for all of them.

The Lincoln family arrived during the fall in a Lexington that had been laid waste by plague. The sights made Mary shudder. Pieces of faded crepe still hung limply from unkempt doorways; the once neat gardens and back yards were filled with litter; alien grass grew untidily on streets and sidewalks.

Even the surrounding countryside, likened so often by contemporary writers to a great parkland, had been blighted by months of neglect. Tobacco rotted where it stood in the fields; the entrances of once trimly kept estates were overgrown.

Betsy and Mary were on friendly terms, the Lincolns visiting her at Buena Vista, traveling back and forth to Lexington on the steam cars. Lincoln was already representing the heirs in another case in which Robert S. Todd had been involved before his unexpected death. Ironically it was one in which Mary's father had disputed the validity of a cousin's will.

The Lexington friends were impressed by Lincoln's appearance, for his Washington sojourn had made him more clothes-conscious. He appeared wearing a well-cut black frock coat, broadcloth pantaloons, choker-style black cravat, high moleskin hat, and a short circular blue coat. He was quite as smartly attired as any of the other well-dressed Lexington lawyers.

A *Death in the Family* : : *page 59*

While on this second short trip to Lexington, Lincoln became more closely acquainted with the horrors of slavery. While the inhabitants eased their consciences with the thought that slavery was sanctioned by Holy Writ, a whipping-post was in constant use in the courthouse yard. Vermin-infested slave coops with their ghastly, often disease-ridden occupants could be seen in the yard of the infamous Pullum's jail. A certain Lewis C. Robards, known as the leading Negro buyer, had leased the Pullum property. He had also obtained the use of the old Lexington Theater where more select human specimens were sold upon the stage.

Some of the slaves were so genteel in manners that they could be seen working away at their needlework and embroidery. The degradation suffered by these unfortunate creatures at the physical examinations forced upon them before prospective buyers was unthinkable.

Betsy agreed that a suit should be brought by herself as administratrix of Robert's estate so that his debts might be paid, and the holdings sold. The remaining monies would then be distributed as the court had ordered. Mary and Abraham were able to leave for Springfield by November 10. Sickened by the family squabbling and the atmosphere of slavery, they were not sorry to go.

It was during December that little Eddie first took ill. Mary noticed that the child, usually so energetic, had suddenly become sluggish. In the middle of playing he would crawl upon her lap and go to sleep. He complained of a pain in his throat which, upon examination, was found to be very inflamed. Mary's uncle, Dr. Todd, was duly sent for who, after a thorough examination announced to the startled parents that the child was starting diphtheria.

With orders to swab the child's throat every four hours with a solution made from twenty grains of nitrate of silver dissolved in an ounce of water, for five days the parents were without proper sleep. They used a little sponge attached to a piece of whalebone for Eddie's treatment.

At last the crisis passed and with it Christmas and the New Year. They thought that Eddie was getting stronger. Then late

A Rose for Mrs. Lincoln : : *page 60*

in January he again worsened; his soft palate and pharynx became paralyzed. Next day his sight became affected and paralysis crept down all one side of his small body. Early on February 1, 1850, Eddie Lincoln died. Mary and Abraham had nursed him for fifty-two days. Mary could not bear to see him laid in the ground, so Abraham followed the little coffin to the cemetery alone.

CHAPTER SIX

CIRCUIT DAYS

With heavy heart Mary bade Abraham goodbye as he left to ride the circuit in his ramshackle, one-horse buggy pulled by "Old Buck," described by his fellow lawyer and friend, Henry C. Whitney, as an "indifferent, raw-boned specimen." "Old Buck" lived in a rough stable in the back yard of the Lincoln home, near the privy and woodpile. Getting Abraham ready for the journey was no small feat for, away from Washington's civilizing influence, he had lost no time in sliding back to his previous indifference to both clothes and personal appearance. Once, in court, he confessed that he had never paid more than twenty-eight dollars for a suit in his life. His ill-fitting, swallow-tailed broadcloth cloak was seldom brushed unless Mary did it herself. In bright light it was positively rusty. His trousers were always too short; the nap of his tall brown hat was worn off. He never troubled to blacken or grease his boots, and the high-neck stock was seldom renewed. He refused to buy a new carpet bag, and the striped one he carried was as dilapidated-looking as his enormous faded green umbrella. He loved this umbrella, having asked Mary to sew his name, cut from white muslin, inside. The knob of this favorite accessory had long since been lost, and a piece of string kept it from flapping open. When the weather was cold Abraham wore that same short, circular blue cloak which he had purchased in Washington in 1849, using it regularly for the next ten years. "Whether," says Whitney, "they [his clothes] fitted or looked well was entirely above, or beneath, his comprehension."

In spite of Mary's pleadings, her husband would still answer the door without either a coat or the well-worn stock, which he removed as soon as he reached home. His trousers were held in place with a single suspender that was the amusement of the neighbors when, often in his flapping, homemade slippers, he went to borrow a necessity for the supper table.

Inside the carpet-bag was an extra-long yellow flannel undershirt Mary made for him to sleep in. This ungainly garment reached to his calves. A young lawyer, chancing to see Lincoln so dressed for bed, described the wearer as "the ungodliest figure I ever saw."

Lincoln carried his letters and papers inside his hat as he traveled from township to township, wherever a court might convene. In warm weather he was never without his long white duster coat, under which he wore no other jacket. Sam Alschuler, a photographer, wanting to photograph him upon the circuit, was obliged to lend Lincoln a black coat with a velvet collar before he considered his subject presentable enough to pose.

As court was held in the different counties of Illinois from mid-March until mid-June and again from early September until the first of December, Lincoln was away from home a good deal. Naturally his wife was lonely and his prolonged absences began to irritate her.

For the first three years following his term in Congress, Lincoln "worked" the Eighth Circuit, comprising fourteen counties, in all 140 miles long by nearly 110 miles broad. The Circuit was presided over by Judge David Davis, an enormous figure standing six feet tall and weighing about 320 pounds. The judge needed two horses to pull his buggy, and they were hard put to do so. He became such a staunch friend that Lincoln, in case of his own death, appointed the judge administrator of his small estate.

Whitney speaks of the county seats as being "small and primitive villages" with "unkempt courtrooms, where, ten months in the year, the town boys played at marbles or rudimentary circus." Each town could boast from 500 to 1,000 inhabitants, with a courthouse and jail usually built of logs. Lincoln and his fellow traveling lawyers met with clients on the sunny side of the courthouse on cool days, or under a tree when it was warm. Everyone, from prisoners to judge, had to wash in the same tin basin and use the same towel.

On December 21, 1850, a snowy winter's day, the Lincolns' third son, William Wallace Lincoln, was born. He was so like her little lost Eddie that Mary cried at the first sight of him.

Mary developed milk fever with a temperature of 104 degrees and for a whole month could not leave her bed. Dr. William Wallace, her brother-in-law, had been so faithful in attending her that William, or "Willie" as he soon became known in the family circle, was named for him.

While Abraham was away, Mary carried on with the daily chores and the raising of their boys. The Lincoln cow, bought to provide fresh milk for the children, was a perpetual source of annoyance, for daily it had to be tethered upon a grassy spot in the street. Often the cow would somehow break loose and wander off in search of more juicy pasture. With "Old Buck" and the cow temporarily out of the yard, the Lincoln menagerie consisted of only two pet cats.

Springfield steadily grew in size and activities, and Mary continued to find it a pleasant place in which to live. There were now over 19,000 books in the public library; the two weekly newspapers had become dailies. Every twelve hours, six flour mills ground up 15,000 bushels of wheat. However, the streets were still unpaved and unlighted. Hogs wallowed in the rutted mudholes right in front of the houses, often refusing the right of way to hard-pressed pedestrians. There was no drainage. Ashes, discarded clothing, manure, and other garbage were all thrown into the streets. Nobody then realized that insects spread disease. Flies flew straight from the offal piles into the houses, where the inhabitants brushed them from the mealtables with branches of leaves.

Mary Lincoln was considered "odd" because she indulged in so many baths at home, which were thought unnecessary, although the City Hotel advertised those same sumptuous "Bathing Rooms" which Abraham patronized. Doctors still bled patients, often unnecessarily, using septic and sometimes rusty lancets to cut the veins.

Abraham was at home in Springfield when his father died, January 17, 1851, but Mary was indisposed and he could not go to see the old man before he passed away. "My business is such," wrote Abraham to Harriet Hanks, the granddaughter of his stepmother, Sarah Bush Lincoln, "that I could hardly leave home now, (even) if it was not as it is, that my own wife is sick-a-bed. (It is a case of baby-sickness, and I suppose is not dangerous.) I sincerely hope father may recover his health; but if not, let him put his trust in God."

When the Lincolns did entertain, which wasn't often, Bob, and later the other children, were brought in to dance, recite poetry, and—according to one unappreciative guest—"to show off generally."

Abraham, who idolized Bob, was indifferent to his failings, while Mary, like many mothers, boasted of his accomplishments. "These children may be something sometime," hopefully declared their proud father, "if they are not merely rare-ripes, rotten ripes —hothouse plants. I have always noticed that a rare-ripe child quickly matures, but rots as quickly."

Both parents were blind to Bob's faults, and in an age when corporal punishment was universal, Abraham never punished him. He seemed, for instance, to be oblivious to Bob's rudeness: when his father was playing chess with Justice Samuel Hubbel Treat of the Supreme Court, and had forgotten to come in to dinner, Bob deliberately kicked the board from the players' knees, scattering the chessmen in all directions. Abraham only laughed, then accompanied the boy to eat without one single word of protest. The Judge was furious.

The Lexington lawsuits in connection with the settling of Mary's father's estate still dragged on. In October, 1852, there was much dissention as to the disposition of the slaves. George Todd contended that they had been appraised too low, while the widow Betsy considered their values excessive. Even Chaney, the much-loved cook, together with her six-year-old daughter and six-week-old son were valued in all at $950, which Betsy, wishing to keep them as members of the household, would have been hard put to pay. Betsy contended that Harvey's face was badly scarred, while Pen, who had lived with Levi, had been whipped so much that he was now "delicate and subject to a bleeding of the nose." George had seized the slaves on the pretext that they were "badly clothed and destitute of bed clothing." He was later ordered by the court to return them for sale by public auction at the courthouse door in Lexington.

In spite of such family problems there was joy again in the Lincolns' own small family circle when, on April 4, 1853, Mary gave birth to her fourth son, Thomas. Abraham immediately nicknamed the child "Tadpole," which was soon shortened to Tad. Tad had blond hair and small features. Mary still wished that he might have been her longed-for girl.

Even though the Todd will controversy was terminated, Lincoln found himself personally involved in another case. He was away working the circuit, so it was some time before he received the news that on May 12, 1853, Robert S. Todd's two partners, Oldham and Hemingway, had issued a writ against him.

The plaintiffs claimed that during his father-in-law's lifetime Lincoln had collected various monies from Todd's Illinois cotton customers, converting it to his own use. Lincoln was as outraged as Mary at such accusations, and was completely exonerated when the plaintiffs themselves withdrew the charges. However, they left a bitter taste in his mouth, particularly as he knew Levi Todd to be responsible for the unwarranted action. Lincoln and Ninian W. Edwards had sued Levi, Mary's brother, a few weeks previously, although the nature of the action has been lost. Levi retaliated by getting his father's former partners to file a suit against Lincoln.

Lincoln's vindication came at a time when he was becoming restless to return to political life. The slavery question was again bothering his conscience; the indignity of the enforced sale of Chaney and her children had deeply grieved Mary. When he was not away working the circuit they discussed the sordid question that Stephen A. Douglas had clearly raised by sponsoring the controversial Kansas–Nebraska Bill. The compromise measures advocated by Henry Clay were forgotten when the bill became law.

The Northern newspapers were quick in their condemnation of the new law, which opened as slave territory an area equal to that covered by the thirteen original states.

Lincoln, along with many other inhabitants of Illinois, felt impelled to act quickly.

> I was losing interest in politics when the repeal of the Missouri Compromise aroused me again, but upon that event, I became convinced that either I had been resting in a delusion or the institution was being placed on a new basis—a basis for making it perpetual, national and universal.

Men of good will in Illinois invited the stormy Cassius M. Clay to voice their feelings. When he arrived in Springfield to speak, Clay was refused use of the State House rotunda, so the meeting was held in open woodland near the city. Clay began by likening himself to John the Baptist preaching in the wilderness, pointing out that even in his own slave state of Kentucky, no courthouse or State House had shut its doors in his face. Lincoln, who was at the meeting, listened closely to all the great man had to say. Of that day Clay later recalled,

> Whittling sticks as he lay on the turf, Lincoln gave me a most patient hearing. I shall never forget his long, ungainly form, and his ever sad and homely face. He was but little known to the world, but his being the husband of my old friend of earlier days caused me to look with interest upon him. I flatter myself, when Lincoln listened to my animated appeals for universal liberty for more than two hours, that I sowed good seed in good ground, which in the providence of God produced in time good fruit.

Simeon Francis, editor of the *State Journal* and husband of the matchmaking lady who had once reconciled the estranged Abraham and Mary, estimated that 1,500 people had attended the woodland oratory. A "great heroic speech," he called it.

Lincoln, with his wife's full encouragement, now came to the conclusion that the days of compromising with the slavery adherents were over, for slave extension into the territories that were not yet states must be prevented at all costs. Stephen A. Douglas,

Circuit Days : : *page 67*

nicknamed "Little Giant," now the darling of the South, returned to his Illinois constituents ready to defend his actions in pushing the Kansas–Nebraska Bill. There awaiting him was a somewhat ungainly knight without armor. Abraham Lincoln had quietly put away his law books and girded himself for the battle.

CHAPTER SEVEN

A WISH COME TRUE

"Mr. Douglas is a very little, *little* giant by the side of my tall Kentuckian, and intellectually my husband towers above Douglas just as he does physically." Mary Todd Lincoln spoke of Douglas from first-hand knowledge, as he had once been one of her suitors. Mary's sister Elizabeth had prophesied that Stephen Douglas would go far, yet Mary, to her chagrin, refused him.

In October, 1853, Lincoln, urged by his wife to pit his strength against Douglas at Springfield's State Fair, replied to the pro-slavery speech Douglas made the previous day. They were to meet again twelve days later in joint debate at Peoria. Here Lincoln's simple analysis of the situation assured him of the support of all the anti-slavery forces in Illinois.

Lincoln was now more than ever absorbed in the explosive situation that was threatening the dissolution of the Union and, again urged by Mary, began "mousing about the library of the State House" patiently searching out facts concerning all historical aspects of the slavery question. A volume entitled *Scrap Book on Law and Politics, Men and Times* was presented him by its author, Judge George Robertson of Lexington, and this he found immensely helpful in verifying facts.

Sadly Abraham watched the disintegration of the Whig Party. Then on May 29, 1856, at the Bloomington State Convention, the Republican Party in Illinois came into existence. Casting his lot with the new party, Lincoln made his famed "Lost Speech," which so delighted listening reporters that they forgot to take it down!

A Wish Come True : : *page 69*

By June 16, 1858, when the State Republican Convention met at Springfield, its delegates resolved that "Abraham Lincoln is the first and only choice of the Republicans of Illinois for the United States Senate as the successor of Stephen A. Douglas." Replied Abraham in accepting the nomination,

> A house divided against itself cannot stand. I believe this government cannot endure permanently half slave and half free. I do not expect the Union to be dissolved—
> I do not expect the house to fall—but I do expect it will cease to be divided. It will become all one thing, or all the other.

Handicapped by the political patronage that Senator Douglas had so long controlled, Lincoln declared,

> All the anxious politicians of his party, or who have been of his party for years past, have been looking upon him certainly, at no distant date, to be the President of the United States. . . . On the contrary nobody has ever expected me to be President. In my poor, lean, lank face, nobody has ever seen any cabbages sprouting out. These are disadvantages all taken together that the Republicans labor under. We have to fight this battle on principle and upon principle alone.

Between August 21 and October 15, 1858, Douglas and Lincoln met in Illinois at Ottawa, Jonesboro, Freeport, Charleston, Galesburg, Alton, and Quincy. Although the Chicago *Times* tried its best to ridicule Lincoln out of the race by calling him such things as a "poor desperate creature," it was unsuccessful.

For these debates, Douglas arrived in a procession reminiscent of a conquering hero. Accompanied by his beautiful wife, he even had a booming cannon to announce his arrival. Katherine Helm, Mary Lincoln's niece, writes,

> It is said that Douglas spent no less than $50,000 in
> this canvass. Mr. Lincoln, who thought that he had been

extravagant to spend five hundred dollars, traveled modestly, sometimes even on a caboose or freight train, but as he hated "fireworks, fizzle gigs", this mode of travel suited him better. Mrs. Lincoln stayed quietly at home and kept the home fires burning, trained her children, and read accounts of the speeches in the papers.

In Charleston, Illinois, Lincoln's carriage was followed by a wagon filled to overflowing with thirty-one pretty girls, each representing a state. Their banner read,

Westward the Star of Empire takes its way,
Thy girls Link-on to Lincoln,
Their mothers were for Clay.

On his return home to Springfield, Mary was particularly shocked and disgusted to discover that three of her earliest friends had written letters endorsing Douglas over Lincoln: United States Senator John J. Crittenden, John C. Breckinridge, and, most upsetting, James B. Clay, son of Henry Clay. These false friends were credited with losing Lincoln the election, held November 3 in pouring rain. Crittenden, Mary's father's lifetime friend, had even been best man at his wedding. While Lincoln took his defeat calmly, Mary was more than vocal in her caustic lashing of those three who had betrayed them. She did not know that Lincoln had written Senator Crittenden

> The emotions of defeat at the close of a struggle in which I felt more than a mere selfish interest, and to which defeat the use of your name contributed largely, are fresh upon me; but even in this mood I cannot for a moment suspect you of anything dishonorable.

Lincoln might have lost the Senatorial election, but the people did not forget him. Coming home one evening with a worried look upon his face, he confessed to Mary that in spite of his "poor . . . lank face" there was talk of his being considered as a candidate for the Presidency.

A Wish Come True : : page 71

When he spoke of others such as William H. Seward, United States Senator and former governor of New York, whom he considered more worthy of the honor, and of all the opposition, personal abuse, and hard names they had endured, she replied, "Oh, if abuse is all that is needed to earn the Presidency I think you have earned part of the price already."

Later, Lincoln warmed more to the idea. Cassius Clay, a true friend, stumped central Kentucky for him. On April 4, 1860, proslavers erected a cannon from Lexington in the public square of Richmond, Kentucky, determined to keep Clay out. Not to be intimidated, Clay arrived armed with two big navy revolvers and a bowie knife, shouting for his enemies to shoot him through the head. According to the New York *World*, due to this show of bravery many Union men declared for Lincoln that day.

Shortly after, in Chicago, at the Republican convention which assembled on May 16, 1860, Lincoln was nominated on the third ballot. At home in Springfield, Mary and he were under great tension and strain as they waited for news. Dividing his time between their home and the telegraph office, Lincoln had just left the latter to do some shopping for Mary when the shout went up, "Lincoln is nominated!" Surrounded by elated supporters, his first thoughts were for Mary.

"My friends," he said, his voice filled with emotion, "I am glad to receive your congratulations, and as there is a little woman on Eighth Street who will be glad to hear the news, you must excuse me until I inform her." The little woman on Eighth Street was overcome by the news. "Lincoln was proud of his wife and that he had realized her faith in his star" writes Katharine Helm of their meeting.

All that night happy crowds of wellwishers thronged the streets of Springfield, shouting and singing their rollicking campaign songs. Mary's head began to throb, heralding the approach of one of her sick headaches. The bright glow of the victory bonfires burned her tired eyes, and there was to be no sleep for either of them that night. Judge Stephen T. Logan, her staid cousin, arrived home from the Republican Convention wearing a ridiculous little plaid Scottish cap. The beautiful tall silk hat he had worn so proudly on leaving Springfield had been beaten to a pulp by overly exuberant delegates.

Next morning visitors began to arrive, bearing more congratulations. Mary had begun early cutting sandwiches, which were placed on the large dining room table together with two pitchers of ice water. They had served no liquor since first setting up housekeeping together, and Abraham saw no reason why they should change their temperance habits now. She wondered ironically what her whisky-loving Kentucky ancestors would have said.

She had to have more help, for those who arrived at mealtime stayed late into the evening. Being the wife of the Presidential nominee meant plenty of extra work; the last of the day's guests never seemed to leave before midnight. Then Mary would sleep a few hours, rising again at daybreak to change the flowers that decorated her table. Sometimes her sisters came in to help. Elizabeth Edwards seemed pleased at the Lincolns' good fortune, although her husband was committed to support Abraham's rival, Stephen Douglas. It was a blessed relief that Mary's sister Ann stayed away, for her short temper was uncongenial in a crowd. "The most bad-tempered member of the family" was how a contemporary described her.

Elizabeth Todd Grimsley, bridesmaid at Mary's wedding, made a splendid assistant hostess, and even did the extra marketing. She too was genuinely happy at Mary's good fortune.

A month later the Democrats, meeting in Baltimore, chose two candidates to oppose Lincoln: the Northern faction selected Stephen Douglas, and the Southern, Vice President John C. Breckinridge, who would be running on a slavery platform.

With tongue in cheek Mary listened to some of the election names they were calling Abraham: Honest Abe, Old Abe and some even the Rail Splitter. Somebody had recalled that back in 1830 Lincoln and Thomas Hanks had made 3,000 rails!

When he was not in his office, Lincoln remained at home with Mary during campaign time, when election fever ran high. The governor's office in Springfield had been lent him for the campaign, where on August 8 over fifty thousand Republicans gathered for a great rally.

A Wish Come True

> Ain't I glad I joined the Republicans,
> Joined the Republicans,
> Joined the Republicans,
> Ain't I glad I joined the Republicans,
>   Down in Illinois!

So ran their raucous campaign song.

Cassius M. Clay, together with other ardent Lincoln supporters, was out in the field working vigorously for his man. Eagerly Abraham and Mary followed the stories of their speechmaking and reception in the newspapers. Wellwishers knitted Abraham so many pairs of extra large socks and made him so many pieces of wearing apparel that he could not resist the temptation to quip, "Well, wife, if nothing else comes out of this scrape, we are going to have some new clothes."

November 6, 1860, Election Day, came at last. Lincoln hurried down to his office where he was too excited to answer any of the pile of letters awaiting him. Mary's nerves were so on edge that morning that she nearly scalded herself with the coffee. As telegrams started arriving, repeatedly announcing Lincoln's majority, she became too excited to stay in the house any longer. Hurrying downtown, she joined other Republican ladies who were cooking what they hoped would be a victory supper in the Watson's Saloon. Their suspense lasted until a few minutes after midnight, when the news was telegraphed to Springfield that Lincoln was the new President-elect.

By this time Mary was unable to control her emotions. When Lincoln brought her the news she completely broke down, throwing herself into his arms "in a passion of tears." He knew just how to soothe her when she was in this state. "There, there, little woman," he whispered, "I thought you wanted me to be President."

CHAPTER EIGHT

WIFE OF THE PRESIDENT-ELECT

There was so much to be done. Mary had always wanted to travel, and now had come the opportunity, for the President-elect planned to visit America's main cities. There was also the move from Springfield to Washington. She was quite willing to sell the house, for surely, when he had served out his term as Chief Executive, he would not want to return to a small law practice in Springfield? Even before his Presidential nomination, New York Central Railroad had offered him the handsome sum of ten thousand dollars a year to be their counsel. But Lincoln was adamant. Springfield was his home and to Springfield he would return. Life with Mary had given him roots to which, even though he might be living in the White House, he would always cling.

D. W. Bartlett, correspondent for the New York *Evening Post*, sent to find out what the future First Lady was really like, wrote,

> I had the pleasure . . . of a brief interview with Mrs Lincoln. . . . Whatever of awkwardness may be ascribed to her husband, there is none of it in her. On the contrary, she is quite a pattern of lady-like courtesy and polish. She converses with freedom and grace, and is thoroughly *au fait* in all the little amenities of society.
> . . . [She] has received a liberal and refined education, and should she ever reach it, will adorn the White House.

Mrs. Abraham Lincoln and her sons, William and Thomas. *From the collections of the Library of Congress.*

The preparation of a guest list of relatives and friends to invite to the Inauguration ceremonies was not easy, for few of her own Kentucky relatives had supported him. In all of Lexington there had been only two votes cast for Lincoln.

The younger boys would be going to live in the White House at an age when they most needed their parents' care. Willie was ten years old; Tad nearly eight. Tad had a speech impediment caused by a cleft palate, so that only the immediate family could fully understand what he said.

Robert was away at college. For months Mary had tutored him for the entrance examinations to Harvard. Abraham had been against his application but she had insisted. Learning had always come so easily to Mary that it was hard for her to comprehend that one of her own children might have difficulty. When Robert failed fifteen of the sixteen questions she was mortified. Finally the Harvard people offered the hope that if Robert attended Phillips Exeter Academy in New Hampshire for one year of special tuition he would most likely pass his university examinations. Robert quickly settled down at Exeter, showing little sign of homesickness, which was unusual in a boy who had been so indulged and spoiled at home. With his father's election as President he found his popularity was increasing, as the following letter shows:

> Phillips Exeter Academy.
> December 2, 1860.
>
> Dear Mother:
> You see I am back at Exeter and I feel very much at home. I am here with Dick McConkey. We have been in a constant round of dissipation since we came. On Thursday we were at dinner at Miss Gales, on Friday Mr. Tuck gave a large party which passed off very finely. Mr. Tuck thinks of going to Chicago in about three weeks and thence to St. Louis, so look out for him. To-night we are invited out to tea which will wind up our fun, as we have to commence study again tomorrow. We have only about six weeks more before going home. I see by the papers that you have been to Chicago. Aren't you beginning to get a little tired of this constant uproar? I have a couple of friends, who are

going to the inauguration after vacation is over and I have invited them to stop at our house on their road. They are nice fellows and have been with me for the last year. You will remember that I wrote to father about a fellow who is boring me considerably. He capped the climax lately. There was a Republican levee and supper at Cambridge to which I was invited. I did not go for I anticipated what really happened. I was sitting in my room about 6:30 when two boys came in and handed me an admission ticket, on the back of which the fellow had written asking me to come over as they were calling for me. I wrote him a note excusing myself. He must be the biggest fool in the world not to know I did not want to go over, when if I did I would be expected to make a speech! Just phancy my phelinks mounted on the rostrum holding "a vast sea of human faces, etc." I stop overwhelmed.

> Yours affectionately,
> R. T. LINCOLN.

His parents had left for Chicago just two weeks after the election, where it had been arranged that Lincoln should meet the Vice President-Elect, Hannibal Hamlin of Maine. Standing in line with Mary and Hamlin at the Tremont House, he shook hands for two hours and a half.

Wellwishers noticed that he had started to grow a beard, something that many had been begging him to do in order to look more "dignified." A little girl named Grace Bedell of Westfield, New York had written him,

> I have got four brothers and part of them will vote for you anyway and if you will let your whiskers grow I will try to get the rest of them to vote for you. You would look a great deal better for your face is so thin. All the ladies like whiskers and they would tease their husbands to vote for you and then you would be President.

With some amusement he had replied, "As to the whiskers, having never worn any, do you not think people would call it a piece of silly affectation if I were to begin now?"

On January 10, Mary, in the company of several friends and her merchant brother-in-law, C. M. Smith, made a short trip to New York to buy some new dresses, thinking that was where Miss Harriet Lane, niece and ward of outgoing President James Buchanan, and the Washington beauties that clustered around her, bought theirs. Actually they had their dresses sent from Paris. Although in Springfield she had made her own dresses, or employed the best dressmakers she could find, she now desired clothes worthy of a First Lady. In this capacity she was readily given credit and courtesy by A. T. Stewart and other prominent New York merchants. She bought silks for dresses, as well as ornaments and jewelry, and this was the first recorded instance of her obtaining finery upon credit.

Mary Todd Lincoln had never previously shown such poor judgment in money matters, but now her purchases stretched her new-found credit to the breaking point. In the next four years her passion for shopping turned into a financial nightmare. She even bought lace curtains for the White House.

By comparison, Lincoln—completely unaware of this new trait in his wife's character—knew no such financial worries from the moment he entered the White House. He owned some real estate, plus an accumulation of good liquid assets which, with his Presidential salary of twenty-five thousand dollars a year, would go far beyond his simple needs. He still intended to go back to Springfield, where his partner, William H. Herndon, was instructed not to remove the legal plate bearing the Lincoln name.

After a few days in New York Mary went to Cambridge, Massachusetts, where Robert, his year at Exeter having proved successful, had now enrolled at Harvard.

Back home in Springfield with Abraham, Mary arranged a reception for all their friends. A Springfield correspondent of the *Missouri Democrat* described the event in the issue of February 6, 1861.

> The first levee given by the President elect took place last evening at his own residence in this City and it was a

grand outpouring of citizens and strangers together with the members of the Legislature. Your humble servant was invited to attend. Mr. Lincoln threw open his house for a general reception of all the people who felt disposed to give him and his Lady a parting call. The levee lasted from seven until twelve o'clock in the evening, and the house was thronged by thousands up to the latest hour.

Mr. Lincoln received the guests as they entered and were made known. They then passed on and were introduced to Mrs. Lincoln who stood near the center of the parlor and who I must say acquitted herself most gracefully and admirably. She was dressed plainly but richly. She wore a beautiful full trail, white moire-antique silk, with a small French lace collar. Her neck was ornamented with a string of pearls. Her head dress was a simple and delicate vine arranged with much taste. She displayed but little jewelry and this was well and appropriately adjusted.

She is a lady of fine figure and accomplished address and is well calculated to grace and do honor at the White House. She was on this occasion accompanied by four of her sisters—Mrs. W. S. Wallace, Mrs. C. M. Smith of Springfield, Mrs. Charles Kellogg of Cincinnati, and a Miss Todd of Kentucky. They all appeared to be extremely happy and I hope there will be nothing thrown in their way to hinder them from experiencing in full all the pleasures which they now anticipate in coming events. I thought, when looking upon the lovely group of the Todd family, how proud old Kentucky would have felt if she could have been present to witness the position in which her son and daughters were placed. (T. W.)

Not everything connected with this period of waiting for Inauguration Day was so pleasant as the levee. It seemed that the Southern states were now determined to dissolve the Union. On December 20, South Carolina had seceded, a palmetto banner replacing the Stars and Stripes. Early in the New Year she was followed by Mississippi, Florida, Georgia, Alabama, and Louisiana. Texas was to follow later.

A Rose for Mrs. Lincoln : : page 80

With heavy hearts, the Republican President-elect and his Southern-born wife received the news of each defection. Lincoln's life was threatened in anonymous letters boasting that even if he arrived alive in Washington he would be shot before taking the oath of office. With mingled anger and disgust the Lincolns received the mummy of a Negro in a box. Mary opened a package addressed to her to find that it contained a horrible caricature of Abraham, chained, tarred, and feathered, hanging from a tree with a noose around his neck. They leased their house in this atmosphere of emotional tension. Mary's headaches were increasing. At times the pounding in her brain made her raise her voice, which normally she would not have done.

On February 11, 1861, Lincoln was to leave alone on the special Inauguration train, while Mary was to join him later with Willie and Tad. There are differing explanations for this. One is that the veteran General Winfield Scott, head of the army, fearing violence for the Presidential party, thought that she should travel later with the children. Her niece Katherine Helm says that as 8 A.M. was an inconvenient hour, her aunt decided to take a later train, joining the Presidential train in Indianapolis, where it was scheduled to stop all night.

Lincoln's departure from Springfield was a touching and poignant one.

> My friends, no one, not in my situation, can appreciate my feeling of sadness at this parting. To this place, and the kindness of these people, I owe everything. . . . Here my children have been born, and one is buried. I now leave, not knowing when or whether I may return, with a task before me greater than that which rested on Washington.

Mary and the boys joined him next morning in Indianapolis. It was Abraham's birthday and she had bought him a set of silver hair brushes to mark the occasion. Then she made him a little speech, a repetition of that she had made on his birthday after their marriage, "I am so glad you have a birthday. I feel so grateful to your mother." When they were alone he would relax while she carefully combed and brushed his hair.

Wife of the President-Elect : : page 81

The boys were as thrilled as she at the Presidential train, the parlor car of which had been specially designed and built in Buffalo for the occasion. The black walnut furnishings were covered with horsehair upholstery; the carpeting was rich and costly, and the sofa chosen for Lincoln's special use had been built long enough comfortably to accommodate his lanky figure. A refreshment bar added to their pleasure. The train, belonging to the Wabash Railroad, chugged through the Indiana countryside spitting smoke and cinders, at the amazing speed of thirty miles an hour. For the first day, at least, the boys were enthralled by this great adventure, although later, like all youngsters, they became restless.

All along the roadbed little knots of people were gathered to cheer as the train passed. In small towns, crowds stood waiting to greet it, their stations gay with red, white, and blue bunting. Whenever the train stopped, Lincoln stepped out onto the back platform to say a few words. At one station a cry went up for a glimpse of the new First Lady. Back inside he went to get her, returning with his wife of five feet and three inches. "Now you see before you the long and short of the Presidency," he told them. She smiled with pleasure as he protectively held her hand.

Aboard the train with the Lincolns were a varied assortment of friends, state politicians, news correspondents, a military escort of four army officers appointed by the War Department, and even some of Mary's relatives. Elizabeth might not have approved her marriage, but she was now on hand to share Mary's triumph. She was accompanied by her two daughters and by Elizabeth Grimsley, Uncle John Todd's daughter. Ninian Edwards, Elizabeth's husband, after having backed the wrong man, tactfully refused the invitation to attend.

The War Department had sent Major David Hunter, a friend of the Lincolns and an anti-slavery paymaster, who had an amazing dyed mustache and chestnut wig; Colonel Edwin V. Sumner, a Cavalry officer from Massachusetts; Captain John Pope, the son of an Illinois judge; and Colonel Elmer E. Ellsworth, a Zouave (firefighter) drillmaster, whose special responsibility was to shepherd Lincoln through the crowds at the stopping places.

There was one young lawyer who considered himself personally responsible for the Lincolns' safety. Associated with Lincoln in circuit-riding days, his name was Ward Hill Lamon of Virginia. Sporting long hair and a drooping mustache, he carried a varied assortment of brass knuckles, a slingshot, knives, and pistols that clattered as he walked. Both the Lincolns were delighted when they found that Lamon had brought along his banjo upon which he played and sang their favorite Negro songs, including the one Abraham liked best, *The Blue Tailed Fly*. At least his singing kept Willie and Tad quiet for a time.

The Lincolns' progress was unhurried, for in Cincinnati, as in Indianapolis, splendid receptions had been arranged in their honor; then on again to another major stop at Columbus and another in Pittsburgh. There the citizens, unalarmed by the threatened dissolution of the Union, demanded—and got—a speech on the tariff.

The special train, preceded by pilot trains, was to face difficulties upon reaching Baltimore, where the cars were drawn separately between the depots. Baltimore, capital of a slave state, was a hotbed of secessionist agitation and notorious for lawless gangs. Samuel M. Felton, president of the Philadelphia, Wilmington and Baltimore Railroad, was worried not only for Lincoln's safety, but for that of the railroad property. He personally engaged the services of a respected Chicago investigator, Allan Pinkerton, a former Scottish barrelmaker who had founded one of the first private detective agencies in America. Pinkerton, also in the employ of Lincoln's Illinois advisers, had cunningly planted spies in Baltimore's military companies and secret societies. Receiving information of plots to sabotage the railroad, Felton placed two hundred armed guards dressed as railroad workmen along the line between the Susquehanna River and Baltimore.

In Harrisburg Lincoln was told of a rumor involving a barber named Fernandina, head of a secret military society, who planned to assassinate him. It was then decided that he should continue the journey to Washington without Mary or his sons, who would travel next day on the special train. Mary, always fearful now for Abraham's safety, was not happy over the arrangement, and a correspondent noted how she finally arrived in the capital "distraught at the separation from her husband." On the Philadelphia train, Abraham Lincoln, the Sixteenth President of the United States, arrived in its capital like a thief in the night, his face hidden by a soft slouched hat, and wearing a muffler and a short, bobtailed overcoat.

Rooms had been engaged for the Lincolns at Willard's Hotel by Thurlow Weed, political manager from New York State. Unfortunately Lincoln's early and secret arrival had caught the hotel staff by surprise. Quickly they had to ask a New York capitalist to give up his suite, which connected with the Lincolns' parlor.

Lincoln had not been really convinced of the necessity of leaving his family, or of arriving in Washington in such an undignified manner. He did, however, harbor a premonition that he was destined to suffer a violent death, never to return alive to Springfield. He had dreamed of seeing a double image of his face reflected in a swinging mirror over a bureau. One face was much paler than the other. Mary was horrified when he told her the story, for she feared the faces were an omen that although Lincoln would be elected to two Presidential terms, he would not live to finish out the second.

When the First Lady arrived at Willard's, Frederick Seward escorted her into the hotel, where the Willard brothers stood to greet her. She later found Abraham sprawled out in an armchair in their suite upstairs. The children immediately climbed onto his lap, begging him to play with them.

It was not a pleasant arrival, for already the threatening letters were following them. Some were even amusing, such as the one to Lincoln that said, "If you don't resign, We are going to put a spider in your dumpling and play the devil with you."

Toward Mary, the women who made up Washington's Southern-dominated society were vitriolic and abusive. Always more like a Southern than a Northern city, the capital was now undergoing a far-reaching change. It was fast becoming an armed camp, and in a short time Mary was confiding to a friend, "Thousands of soldiers are guarding us, and if there is safety in numbers we have every reason to feel secure."

For many years Washington society had been controlled by Southern women who had little time for those whose husbands represented the rest of the country. During that winter many Southern senators and their wives would leave for home. The "aristocrats" who remained looked upon their Southern-born First Lady as a traitor for being married to the champion of anti-slavery, and the leader of a new social revolution. Because of Mary's long residence in Illinois, the Southern women expected to find backwoods manners in the White House. Mary, a proud Kentucky Todd whom Abraham had once teased, "One 'd' is good enough for God, but not for the Todds," never forgave them this slight.

Yankee residents in Washington were equally unkind, for they decided that a Southern spy was destined for the White House! Southerner she might be, but Mary Lincoln was loyal to her husband, believing, like him, that the Union should be preserved intact at all costs.

Bob Lincoln had arrived to join his parents and small brothers at Willard's, where he was described by a contemporary as being the life of the party. He was now adult enough to visit the smoking room downstairs and indulge in a cigar. He enjoyed listening to the harpist's music, but complained when some anti-unionists persuaded them to play "Dixie," now the national air of the seceded Confederacy. Diplomatically they followed it with "Hail Columbia."

Mary, wearing one of her pretty Springfield toilettes, received guests in the parlor of her suite, attended by her sister Elizabeth, her two nieces, and her cousin Elizabeth. Pleased with her new status, she discussed politics openly, just as she had done back in Kentucky. When she became overtired she was still plagued with terrible headaches, at times so painful as to make her hysterical, for which others criticized her for having what they called "tantrums." At these times Abraham simply took the smaller boys by the hand and went out walking, knowing that when they returned she would most likely have recovered. Then he called her "my child-wife."

At a reception, when one guest commented on how often he looked at Mary, Abraham replied, "My wife is as handsome as when she was a girl, and I, a poor nobody then, fell in love with her, and what is more, I have never fallen out."

"If you are as happy, my dear sir, on entering this house as I am on leaving it and returning home, you are the happiest man on earth." This was the greeting awaiting them from outgoing President Buchanan at the White House.

It was not the kind of Inauguration Mary had dreamed of for

Abraham. With a military escort instead of an honorary one, it was unlike any other that had gone before. The intense feeling between North and South marred the occasion, although the large military parade seemed to lend assurance to the nervous Washington populace. To Mary the entire day seemed full of foreboding. One look at President Buchanan's chalk-white face told how sick he was: sick not only in body but of the Presidency. "I am now in my sixty-ninth year," he had written his friend, Sarah Childress Polk, widow of President James Knox Polk, two years previously, "and am heartily tired of my position as president."

Then, driving along Pennsylvania Avenue in a carriage allotted to herself and the boys, Mary could not fail to note the many solemn and unfriendly faces. Ahead of her, Lincoln's carriage was heavily guarded, in front by West Point sappers and miners, and on either side by cavalrymen. Behind were detachments of both militia and navy.

She found herself gazing uneasily upwards to where sharp-shooters had been stationed on roofs and at strategic windows. Her nerves were on edge, waiting for a gunshot that never came. There was scant consolation in General Scott's description of the Inaugural parade as a "movement" designed to repulse any possible invasion of the capital in addition to protecting Lincoln's life.

An air of sadness seemed to prevail as the First Lady, together with her sons, took her seat on the second row of a special platform built out from the Capitol's east portico, for all around were great blocks of granite, tools, and cables, so long neglected that weeds were growing from among them. Lincoln was even inheriting a Capitol building that was unfinished, to say nothing of the Washington Monument, commemorating the father of his country. Only one-third of the shaft of this obelisk had been erected when the subscription drive for its completion was allowed to lapse. Patriotic Americans were forced to pick their way through the high grass and loose, unplaced stonework to see what had been accomplished so far.

Ironically, for the seventh time in his career, Chief Justice Taney, whose Dred Scott decision declared that slaves were not human beings, stepped forward with a cinnamon-velvet-bound Bible to swear in this unpopular Republican President.

Then with pride Mary listened as the incoming President began to read his Inaugural address. As always the threat of civil war was uppermost in his mind.

> In your hands, my dissatisfied fellow countrymen, and not in mine, is the momentous issue of civil war. . . . The government will not assail you. You can have no conflict without being yourselves the aggressors. You have no oath registered in Heaven to destroy the government, while I shall have the most solemn one to "preserve, protect and defend" it. I am loth to close. We are not enemies, but friends. We must not be enemies. . . .
>
> I, Abraham Lincoln, do solemnly swear that I will faithfully execute the office of the President of the United States, and will, to the best of my ability, preserve, protect and defend the Constitution of the United States.

Mary was still half in a dream, carried away by her husband's words, when she realized that he was kissing her, the most solemn kiss of their entire years together. Then the cannon were booming and they were on the way to the White House to watch the Inaugural parade. One of the decorative floats carried thirty-four young girls, each representing a state in the Union. As the float passed the new President, the girls rushed over to him, and he kissed each one of them. "Old Edward" who had served many Administrations, then opened the main doors of the White House to admit the First Family.

That evening Mary's head was so bad that neither she nor Abraham could attend the Inaugural Ball, which was held in a frame building, fantastically dubbed "The White Muslin Palace of Aladdin."

Mary, sensitive to the barbs of the Washington aristocracy that she was vulgar, ignorant, and rude, developed an almost psychopathic passion to possess richer gowns, to outdress them. To her new Negro *modiste* and friend, Elizabeth Keckley, a former slave, she carefully explained, "I must dress in costly materials. The

Elizabeth Keckley, Mary Todd Lincoln's dressmaker, confidante, and friend.

people scrutinize every article that I wear with critical curiosity. The very fact of having grown up in the West subjects me to more searching observation."

Mrs. Keckley had been recommended to the First Lady by a Mrs. McClean who had first sent her up to the Lincolns' suite at Willard's. Says Mrs. Keckley, "With a nervous step I passed on, and knocked at Mrs. Lincoln's door. A cheery voice bade me come in, and a lady, inclined to stoutness, about forty years of age, stood before me."

So began an association between the two women that was to weather both good times and bad. Mrs. Keckley treated the First Lady with loyalty, kindliness, and deference. Mary was reminded of her childhood in the South and was much at ease with the Negro woman. Mrs. Keckley was a most intelligent woman who proved her worth many times afterwards as the First Lady's understanding friend. Mary told her at their first meeting, "I have not time to talk to you now, but would like to have you call at the White House, at eight o'clock to-morrow morning, where I shall then be."

Mrs. Keckley, who for some time had cherished an ambition to work in the President's home, could hardly wait for the next day to come. She was therefore somewhat disappointed when she arrived at eight o'clock the next morning to find three other mantua-makers also waiting for a similar interview.

Mrs. Lincoln was immediately attracted to the fourth and last applicant, especially when she told her that she had worked for Mrs. Jefferson Davis, whose husband would find his place in history as President of the Confederacy. Mrs. Davis had done her best to persuade Mrs. Keckley to go South with the family when they left Washington, telling her somewhat prematurely, "As soon as we go South and secede from the other States, we will raise an army and march on Washington, and then I shall live in the White House."

Encouraged by her new employer's interest, Mrs. Keckley asked the First Lady if she would have much work for her to do.

> That, Mrs. Keckley, will depend altogether upon your prices. I trust that your terms are reasonable. I cannot afford to be extravagant. We are just from the West, and are poor. If

you do not charge too much, I shall be able to give you all my work.... If you will work cheap, you shall have plenty to do. I can't afford to pay big prices, so I frankly tell you so in the beginning.

Mrs. Keckley agreed to the First Lady's rather meager terms and was immediately commissioned to work upon a gown of "a bright rose-colored moiré-antique" for the First Lady to wear at the President's first levee, and for a "waist of blue watered silk for Mrs. Grimsly." The levee was held March 8, and the new First Lady was so nervous that upon Mrs. Keckley's late arrival with the finished gown she became very angry.

"Mrs. Keckley," she grumbled, "you have disappointed me—deceived me. Why do you bring my dress at this late hour?"

"Because I have just finished it, and thought I should be in time," replied Mrs. Keckley very calmly.

"But you are not in time, Mrs. Keckley," complained Mrs. Lincoln. "You have bitterly disappointed me. I have no time now to dress, and what is more, I will not dress, and go downstairs." She pouted.

Mrs. Keckley had no intention of ending their relationship there. She knew just how to coax this highly strung Southern woman out of her baby-like tantrums.

"I am sorry if I have disappointed you, Mrs. Lincoln, for I intended to be in time. Will you let me dress you? I can have you ready in a few minutes."

But Mary was determined to play out her scene. "No, I won't be dressed. I will stay in my room. Mr. Lincoln can go down with the other ladies."

"But there is plenty of time for you to dress, Mary." Sister Elizabeth and Cousin Elizabeth Grimsley now tried their own powers of persuasion. "Let Mrs. Keckley assist you, and she will soon have you ready."

Mrs. Lincoln capitulated. Childlike and submissive, she now allowed Mrs. Keckley to dress her. The gown fitted perfectly. She was delighted. Then the President came in with Willie and Tad. He commenced to put on his gloves, at the same time quoting poetry.

A Rose for Mrs. Lincoln : : page 90

"You seem to be in a poetical mood tonight," said the First Lady.

"Yes, Mother," he replied, using the term of endearment that seems to have replaced the more flippant "Puss." "These are poetical times." He gazed admiringly at her. "I declare, you look charming in that dress. Mrs. Keckley has met with great success."

The First Lady looked elegant in her new gown, complemented with a necklace, earrings, and bracelets of pearls. The favorite red roses adorned her hair. Just before going downstairs upon the President's arm, she discovered her lace handkerchief to be missing. There was a frantic search until it was found; Tad had hidden it!

Mrs. Keckley then tells us,

> The handkerchief found, all became serene. Mrs. Lincoln took the President's arm, and with smiling face led the train below. I was surprised at her grace and composure. I had heard so much, in current and malicious report, of her low life, of her ignorance and vulgarity, that I expected to see her embarrassed on this occasion. Report, I soon saw, was wrong. No queen, accustomed to the usages of royalty all her life, could have comported herself with more calmness and dignity than did the wife of the President. She was confident and self-possessed, and confidence always gives grace.

One of the First Lady's few friends wrote disgustedly,

> Women who knew the wire-pulling at Washington, whose toilet arts and social pretensions, society-lobbying and opportunity-seeking taught them to lie in wait and rise in the social scale by intimacy at the White House, these basely laughed at the credulous woman who took counsel from them. . . . Some said to her, "They say you are a Western woman, and that brilliant life is unknown to you. Prove by your style and splendor that to be Western is not to be a boor."

Wife of the President-Elect : : *page 91*

It was to be some time before Mary realized that all her wild spending upon costly materials for the fancy dresses with which she hoped vainly to win the approval of her enemies in the capital only gave them more to criticize. When she did wake up to the fact, she could only comment "I have been the victim of evil counselors."

CHAPTER NINE

LIFE IN THE WHITE HOUSE

Although strict precautions had been taken to guard the new President's life en route to Washington, now that he was established in the White House nobody seemed to care. Their living quarters were so arranged that, to get from his office to the family dining room and bedrooms, the President had almost to fight his way through lines of eager office-seekers, some of whom actually grabbed his arm in an effort to present their papers. There was little privacy either for himself or for the First Lady. Executive business was carried on in three rooms at the eastern end of the second floor; at the other end of the same hall were the family bedrooms. Even the mentally sick could push their way into his presence.

Their cramped "public" living quarters did not worry Willie or Tad, who romped through the White House from attic to ground floor, sliding down the stair-rails in their daily quest for a good time. Lincoln was still criticized by official visitors for the time he devoted to playing with his young sons.

The family living quarters were indescribably shabby, but no more so than the official East, Blue, and Red Rooms which, according to a contemporary description, were "bare, worn and soiled" so that they looked like "the breaking up of a hard winter about a deserted farmstead." The East Room ran the entire depth of the White House.

Making a hasty tour of these famous rooms where the Administration's formal entertaining would be held, Mary Lincoln was disillusioned by what she saw. Frayed muslin backing glared back at her from dusty East Room hangings; velvet carpets were full of holes; the chandeliers looked as if they had not been washed for years. Paint was peeling off the Oval Room ceiling; the Red Room wallpaper was so discolored that it had faded into brown. It had been ten years since Abigail Powers Fillmore, wife of President Millard Fillmore, had been allotted money, including two hundred and fifty dollars for books, by Congress to start the first permanent White House Library. She had also been allowed to install a coal range in the kitchen. In the bachelor President Buchanan's time the only White House appropriation had been spent upon a conservatory!

Mary was shocked that the nation's first home should be in such a state of dilapidation. Abraham must obtain a Congressional appropriation to remedy the squalid situation. She was full of plans, but they must wait their time, for soon soldiers were camping in the East Room and corridors.

Bud and Holly Taft, sons of Judge and Mrs. Horatio N. Taft, prominent Washington residents, were the special playmates of Willie and Tad, and their sixteen-year-old sister Julia often accompanied them. Mrs. Lincoln tried hard to give her boys a normal upbringing within the goldfish-bowl existence in the White House. To Mrs. Taft she would send a friendly note, "Send them [the children] around tomorrow, please . . . Willie and Tad are so lonely and everything is so strange to them here in Washington." Bud became Willie's special friend, and Holly, Tad's. The boys took turns eating at each other's homes, and on one occasion, while their mother was on a shopping trip, the Taft youngsters stayed at the White House.

Julia adored her visits because Mrs. Lincoln was so unlike her own mother and others living in that staid Victorian era. At a time when young girls simply did not have opinions of their own, Mrs. Lincoln encouraged Julia to speak her mind. During their first encounter the First Lady overcame Julia's shyness by sitting next to her on the sofa, asking questions, and encouraging the girl to open up her heart. All her life Julia never forgot Mary Lincoln, and was one of her most staunch defenders. She remembered that on her first meeting Mrs. Lincoln was "dressed in a fresh lilac organdy and looked very attractive."

When Julia, wearing her first grownup long dress, attended a Presidential levee, the girl was mortified when a huge cavalryman wearing spurs walked on her train. All around her, other guests were noticeably amused, but not the Lincolns, who pretended to see nothing. It was to Mary, not to her mother, that Julia confided the story of her boyfriend who had slipped off to join the Confederates, begging her to fly with him "to the Southern clime." Although Julia had a dread of playing the piano for anybody else, she found reassurance with the First Lady turning the music sheets.

Often Julia was called upon as a reinforcement when the four boys had the President pinned to the floor. "Julie, come quick and sit on his stomach," they would all shout, an invitation which she declined. However, when the boys arranged themselves with the President in his large chair, Abraham, putting out a long arm, would draw Julia into the intimate group.

The Lincoln boys preferred attending Julia's church more than their own because it was "lots livelier." Tad was no angel to take to church as Julia soon found out. Once he borrowed a knife from a young officer and promptly cut his finger, which she had to bandage on the spot with her best Sunday handkerchief. When she begged him to be quiet, he answered out loud, "Just you keep your eyes on Willie, sitting there as good as pie." Tad only tolerated church to be with Willie, who loved it. They particularly liked Julia's church because when the preacher prayed for the President, the "seceshes" as Tad dubbed them, immediately left, banging their pew doors behind them.

One night it rained, so the Taft boys stayed over at the White House. Next day Mrs. Taft was shocked to learn that the First Lady had dressed all four youngsters in clean blouses to attend a state dinner. The children sat at the bottom of the table. Tad and Willie were pleased that "Ma was dressed up, you bet," though disappointed that Pa in his black suit looked plain beside the elaborately dressed ambassadors "all tied up with gold cords." Like their father, the Lincoln boys cared little for appearances. Once they visited the Tafts in a rainstorm, carrying a much-battered umbrella hastily borrowed from the cook. Mary dressed them more practically than fashionably, so that Tad was once described as being "rather a

Life in the White House : : *page 95*

grotesque looking little fellow, in his gray trap-door pants made, in true country style, to button to a waist—and very baggy they were." Attired like midwestern children, they looked rather "homely" compared to Washington's society children. Long curls and velvet suits were noticeably missing. No wonder Tad was annoyed at being called a mudsill, though he didn't know what it meant until he asked Julia: "A boy in Lafayette Square said we were 'em and we am not." A mudsill was a slur implying that a person came from a lower social class.

The boys were the recipients of many pets, and the President had a little dog named Jip who never absented himself from his executive master's lunch. He jumped into the President's lap for the first bite of food and was petted throughout the meal. Then there was Nanko the nanny-goat, more popular with the President and his sons than with the gardener, for she was partial to flowers. Tad set Nanko a bad example when he ate up all the strawberries the gardener had forced for a state dinner.

Later when Tad was vacationing with his mother, the President sent them the sad news, "Tell dear Tad, poor 'Nanny Goat' is lost. The day you left, Nanny was found resting herself, and chewing her little cud, on the middle of Tad's bed. But now she's gone!" Nanko never returned. Then there were two other special goats. Says Mrs. Keckley, "Mrs. Lincoln was not fond of pets, and she could not understand how Mr. Lincoln could take so much delight in his goats." Fortunately the President found a fellow goat admirer in Mrs. Keckley. "Madam Elizabeth, you are fond of pets, are you not?" he asked her.

"O yes, sir," she replied enthusiastically.

"Well, come here and look at my two goats. I believe they are the kindest and best goats in the world. See how they sniff the clear air, and skip and play in the sunshine. Whew! what a jump. Madam Elizabeth, did you ever before see such an active goat? He feeds on my bounty and jumps with joy. Do you think we could call him a bounty-jumper? See, Madam Elizabeth," he shouted with all the joy of a young child, "my pets recognize me." And he laughed aloud as they bounded across the White House lawn. Mrs. Lincoln was not so pleased.

Abraham Lincoln and his son, Tad. *From the collections of the Library of Congress.*

"Come 'Lizabeth," she called from a window, "if I am to get ready to go down this evening I must finish dressing myself, or you must stop staring at those silly goats."

Both the President and his wife shared the view that pranks were funny, so Willie's and Tad's daily antics amused rather than annoyed them. The White House roof would become a circus ground with Tad, wearing his father's spectacles, singing "Old Abe Lincoln came out of the wilderness," until Secretary John Hay came rushing into the arena to collect the glasses for their rightful owner. The Lincoln parents later paid five cents each to watch the performance. One wonders if the goats were coaxed into the act?

Then on another exciting occasion the roof became a warship, with a log serving as a cannon, and several old guns that did not work. The Lincoln and Taft boys called their outfit "Mrs. Lincoln's Zouaves." Once they found a gun that would fire, letting it off from an upstairs window of the Taft home and scaring a washerwoman nearly out of her wits. The President and First Lady duly inspected "Mrs. Lincoln's Zouaves," even presenting it with a flag.

Tad disliked photographers as much as his mother did. She hated sitting still for so long, and once ordered all photographs of herself to be destroyed. Tad had his own personal reasons for disliking them. Once a group visiting the White House to photograph his father were shown into a room to develop their efforts, not knowing it had already been commandeered by Tad for a little theater. He was furious, locking the door so they could not get their chemicals which were already inside. They had no business in his room, he insisted, and refused to let them in. It took a visit from his father to get the key. Apologizing to the harassed photographers, the President explained, "Tad is a peculiar child. He was violently excited when I went to him. I said, 'Tad, do you know you are making your father a great deal of trouble?' He burst into tears, instantly giving me up the key." From long experience the father knew that in dealing with both younger children or their mother, an affectionate appeal brought the quickest response.

Tad, like his mother, liked to acquire and hoard things. Julia noted that if her brothers and the Lincoln boys started out with the same number of marbles in the morning, it was always Tad who had them all by nightfall. When the President gave orders for a national fast day, Tad was so upset that he took food from the White House kitchen to stock up his own private larder under a carriage seat in the coach house. The President was much amused when he found out, declaring, "If he grows to be a man, Tad will be what the women all dote on—a good provider."

Tad's mother was a possessive wife who liked to wait upon her husband, and interfered with household management more than any other First Lady in memory. The White House domestic staff at times deplored her. She was so unpredictable that one White House aide saw fit to write, "The Hell-cat is getting more Hell-cattical day by day." Commissioner of Public Buildings Benjamin Brown French was kinder, though he did think the First Lady eccentric. "Mrs. Lincoln is—Mrs. Lincoln, and nobody else," he decided, "and like no other human being I ever saw. She is not easy to get along with."

William O. Stoddard, whose former duty on the White House office staff was to sign land patents, also found himself in charge of Mrs. Lincoln's mail. The incoming mail had to be carefully screened before she read it, for threatening and highly critical letters still poured in. Stoddard says of Mrs. Lincoln,

> It was not easy at first to understand why a lady who could be one day so kindly, so considerate, so generous, so thoughtful and so hopeful, could upon another day appear so unreasonable, so irritable, so despondent, so even niggardly, and so prone to see the dark, the wrong side of men and women and events.

Niggardly she was, even suggesting that the President make extra money by selling manure from the White House stables.

Her headaches did not abate at all, although when she was free of them she did carry Abraham his meals when he worked late, or when she heard him pacing the floor in the night. He occupied the small, southwest bedroom while she slept in the larger adjoining one. She coaxed him into taking drives with her in the carriage so that his nerves might be relaxed; she invited old friends from Illinois in for breakfast, still the family meal they had so enjoyed together in Springfield—only here in the White House

Life in the White House : : *page 99*

she had a better selection of fresh flowers for her centerpiece. She would have tea with him while she read a poem or quotations that he liked from the Bible. Sometimes the President did the reading while she knitted quietly beside him. From the beginning of their tenure of the White House, Mary Todd Lincoln tried hard to lighten her husband's great burden.

CHAPTER TEN

THE FIRST FAMILY

After the firing on Fort Sumter by the Confederates on April 12, 1861, and the secession of Virginia, Washington resembled a city under siege. For the Confederacy to have captured the capital, symbol of the Union, would have earned them enormous prestige and recognition abroad. It would not be easy to defend the capital city, sprawling in its marshy valley, having for protection only one neglected fort twelve miles down the Potomac. Washington relied on manpower.

The Lincolns, already driven half-crazy by the never-ending stream of office seekers who pestered the President even when he was trying to go to bed, now had to contend with the noise of soldiers drilling and camping beneath the great chandeliers in the East Room. Led by General Jim Lane from Kansas, a sad-faced man with noticeably bad teeth, was a motley collection of jayhawkers together with some Easterners wearing civilian clothes. They all had new muskets, while General Lane proudly brandished a sword. When these Frontier Guards, as they called themselves, had finished their drill practice, they rolled up on the carpets to sleep.

The city shop windows were shuttered; all places of amusement and some offices were closed. The big hotels like Willard's were almost empty. Food came by rail through the hostile state of Maryland, prompting some dishonest merchants to speculate on their foodstuffs. Flour rose quickly from seven and a half dollars to fifteen dollars a barrel.

The First Family :: page 101

The President's nerves were on edge; only the First Lady, with her patience and understanding, seemed able to dispel his gloom. Out walking one day he actually found the doors of the Arsenal open. Anyone could have helped himself to arms.

Lincoln's proclamation had called for the enlistment of 75,000 militiamen for a term of three months. Slowly the trains began to arrive at the Washington depot with volunteers from all parts of the country. The Washington Artillery of Pottsville had brought with them an aged Negro, Nick Biddle, who enjoyed going on outings. This time he had donned a uniform for the excursion, only to find instant fame as the first war casualty to enter Washington. Stoned by a mob as the train passed through Baltimore, his head had been hit and bloodied. He told onlookers at the depot that he was not afraid to fight, but that he never wanted to go through Baltimore again!

With a spyglass one could glimpse a Confederate flag flying from the roof of Marshall House, a tavern across the Potomac in Alexandria, while at night the campfires of General Robert E. Lee's forces sparkled like glowworms along the Virginia side of the shore.

Young Colonel Elmer E. Ellsworth, head of the Chicago Zouaves, who had trained them primarily for firefighting in their native city, and who had been a bodyguard on the Lincoln Presidential train, was shot while tearing down the Marshall House flag. The Lincolns, feeling his untimely death to be a personal loss, had Ellsworth's body lie in state in the East Room, where thousands filed past to pay their last respects. The First Lady placed a spray of white lilies upon his breast and, on top of the casket, his picture framed by a waxen laurel wreath. She had been deeply moved by the tale that a round golden medal inscribed *"Non nobis, sed pro patria"* had been driven into his heart by the death shot.

With Lincoln dubbed "The Abolitionist" on one side, and with her four brothers and three brothers-in-law active in the service of the Confederate Army, the First Lady was in a most distressing position. Not only was Mrs. Lincoln reviled by her native South, but by reason of that birth she was distrusted by the North. The Northerners had little need to doubt her, for Mary Todd Lincoln was absolutely in accord with all her husband's policies, and had from childhood been opposed to slavery. To the unhappy

First Lady, Washington seemed to be a city of nothing but hate. While the crowds were singing, "We'll hang Jeff Davis on a Sour Apple Tree," she had heard that in the South Lincoln's name was being used as a substitute. Whenever the First Lady's carriage approached, a certain young Southern girl flung up her windows, rushed to her piano, and sang "Dixie."

A staunch friend in these times was—of all people—Mrs. Stephen A. Douglas, whose husband, the "Little Giant," had opposed Lincoln in the famous debates. Mrs. Douglas often received with Mrs. Lincoln at the White House, which gave great offense to many Republican women, Douglas himself being the Democratic leader. Unfortunately, he was to die June 3, 1861.

Those of Mary's relatives who visited the Lincolns sometimes found it to be an embarrassing experience, as in the case of her half-sister Martha, Mrs. Clement White, known to the family as "Mattie," who was said to be more like Mary than any other member of the Todd family. As she was a great favorite with Lincoln, he gave her a pass which would see her safely through the Northern lines. On one visit to the White House, she decided to leave her trunk, known as a Saratoga, in a Washington hotel with two Baltimore friends. It was filled with extra clothes that she would not need. She gave a key to one friend, instructing her to send a particular blue brocaded dress to the White House if she should need it. At the expiration of her visit she called at the hotel for her trunk, to find that her friends, having left for Baltimore, had left the key with the desk clerk. At that moment an officer appeared and demanded to search Mattie's luggage. Indignant, the First Lady's half-sister declared that she had nothing contraband in it. Then proudly she took out her pass. Upon examining this, the officer touched his cap, leaving her without carrying out a search.

Later, to her chagrin, Mattie found that inside the trunk her friends had placed a splendid uniform and sword for General Robert E. Lee. Says Katharine Helm,

> On her arrival at Richmond, Virginia, she [Mattie] at once consulted President Davis, whom she knew as well as she did her brother-in-law—should she carry the sword and uniform back to Washington and deliver them to

President Lincoln? Of course, he need never know, but she would feel dishonest not to tell him about it.

President Davis decided that General Lee should have the sword and the uniform, but Mrs. White was so mortified and worried over the matter, that President Davis, who had for many years been on pleasant terms with Mrs. White's brother-in-law, wrote a personal letter with his own hand, to President Lincoln explaining the position of Mrs. White. Mrs. White went with this letter to Washington, and the Great Man at the White House took the incident good-naturedly, twitting Mattie about her indignant lie to the inspector. This was the last time Mrs. White ever saw her brother-in-law or her sister Mary. She and her husband were going immediately south, for their hearts were with the Confederacy.

This contretemps was always a source of regret to Mrs. White, who was entirely innocent of any complicity in passing contraband articles through the lines.

Following the Inauguration ceremonies, Mary's cousin, Elizabeth Todd Grimsley, stayed on at the White House for six months, keeping a careful record of all that happened. She made special note of the worrisome office-seekers who approached the ladies of the family with "marked attention and flattery," hoping they would influence the President on their behalf. Every tenth man of these claimed the distinction of having raised Lincoln to the Presidency. Once, in desperation, he exclaimed, "Save me from my friends."

Elizabeth left touchingly human descriptions of the Lincoln boys, Willie and Tad, who were favorites with the White House staff, from Old Edward the doorkeeper to Stackpole the messenger. Elizabeth says,

> Willie, a noble, beautiful boy of nine years, of great mental activity, unusual intelligence, wonderful memory, methodical, frank and loving, a counterpart of his father, save that he was handsome. He was entirely devoted to Taddie, who was a gay, handsome, merry, spontaneous

fellow, bubbling over with the innocent fun, whose laugh rang through the house, when not moved to tears. Quick in mind, and impulse, like his mother, with her naturally sunny temperament, he was the life, as also the worry of the household. There could be no greater contrast between children.

The First Lady's cousin became especially fond of Willie, who seems to have followed her strict observance of the Sabbath.

That Sabbath, after lunch, Willie sat down at the piano in the Red Room, where there were quite a number of persons, and began strumming some popular air; when opportunity came I said to him, "No one is without example, and as your father's son, I would remember the Sabbath day to keep it holy." "I will" was the answer, and he faithfully kept his word, never even joining the family in their afternoon drives, when he found I preferred remaining at home.

When troops were actually billeted in the White House and encamped between the Executive Mansion and the War Department, Willie and Tad did not lack for amusement. They were frequent visitors to the fighting men who found "Taddie's rollicking ways afforded them quite a diversion." Tad's habit of taking gifts to the "good soldiers," especially fruit from the White House conservatory, was "a frequent source of grief to the care-takers."
One morning Abraham, coming in for a late breakfast, found Tad in tears, and upon asking the cause was told, "Why! Faver, such ungrateful soldiers! When I gave them tracts, and asked them to read them, they laughed loud at me, and said they had plenty of paper to start fires with, and would rather have a 'posey.' " The President tried to comfort the child, but even so it was many days before the soldiers saw Tad again.
Willie had said nothing during this little family scene, his silence lasting for fifteen minutes. His father forbade anyone to disturb him. At length the boy looked up, clasped both hands together, shut his teeth firmly over the under lip and then smiled at

his father who exclaimed, "There, you have it now, my boy, have you not?" Willie nodded. Then the President turned to a guest and explained, "I know every step of the process by which that boy arrived at his satisfactory solution of the question before him, as it is by just such slow methods I attain results." Comments Elizabeth, "What the question was, we never knew, save that it was some scheme by which he could apply a balm to Taddie's wounded feelings."

At one of these visits to the Union Army camps, both boys caught the measles and for two or three weeks were very sick. Elizabeth reports,

> The mother, always over-anxious and worried about the boys and withal not a skillful nurse, was totally unfitted for caring for them. They disliked their attendant maid, and, by degrees I was inveigled into the nursery, and by way of a pet name, was dubbed "Grandmother" though a younger woman than the mother.
>
> But I never regretted the days thus spent, for then I learned to know the depth, tenderness, and purity of Mr. Lincoln's nature, his gentleness and patience. "Kind little words, which are of the same blood as great and holy deeds," flowed from his lips constantly to these sick children, the anxious mother, and all others. These were days to be remembered, as this weary over-burdened man found his way through the crowds which still gathered in every hall, to the room where he knew he would bring comfort, and find us with a fragrant cup of tea, and a tempting lunch ready for him. After eating he would stretch himself upon the couch, with a book in his hand, as often the Bible, as any other, for he felt there was nothing in literature that would compare with poetic Job, Moses the Law Giver, the beautiful and varied experiences of the Psalms of David, or the grand majestic utterances of Isaiah. He would read aloud to us, recite some poem, until recalled to the cares of state by the messenger. And this was, at that time, the only relaxation he took.

A Rose for Mrs. Lincoln : : *page 106*

Just at this time there arrived for the First Lady a present from China, an elegant tea caddy "containing such delicious tea, as only emperors use," and several valuable books of paintings on rice paper, which had been rescued from a burning palace. These books of flowers, birds, and Chinese officials in gorgeous robes were a source of endless amusement to the convalescing Lincoln boys.

CHAPTER ELEVEN

WAR DAYS

The First Lady and the Secretary of State had a spirited argument over the new Administration's first public reception which the Secretary thought he should give. Mary objected strongly, saying that the first official function should be given by none other than the President. Mary Lincoln had her way and the "monstrous gathering," held on April 8, was well attended. Even the oldest White House partygoers declared that it had never been exceeded in brilliance, nor had so many people ever entered the White House at one single time. The great driveway was blocked with carriages an hour before the doors were opened. By 8:30 P.M. the crowd was so great, both inside and out, that for one hour it was necessary for departing guests to leave through the windows! Congressman Charles Francis Adams of Massachusetts noted in his diary,

> A pretty business it was. Such a crush was, I imagine, never seen in the White House before on a similar or any other occasion. . . . It was a motley crowd. There they were—the sovereigns; some in evening dress, others in morning suits, with gloves and without gloves, clean and dirty, all pressing in the same direction and all behaving with propriety.

One Washington hostess who was kindly disposed toward the Lincolns—her precocious little girl, Rose, played with Tad Lincoln

Mary Todd Lincoln. *From the collections of the Library of Congress.*

—was Mrs. Rose O'Neal Greenhow, a Marylander, a Virginian's widow, and the aunt of Mrs. Stephen Douglas. Since the death of her husband, Robert, Mrs. Greenhow had lived in a small house on the corner of Sixteenth Street, right across from St. John's Church. Although no longer young, she was said to be the most "persuasive" woman in Washington. To her cozy parlors, divided by vivid red gauze, came many important visitors, including the great Seward himself. At a party, Mrs. Greenhow—a passionate Southerner—once mixed Republicans with Southerners. Mrs. Charles Francis Adams tactlessly praised John Brown, the fanatical abolitionist, and Mrs. Greenhow promptly denounced her. Mrs. Greenhow was in fact a spy, listening with keen ears to all her guests' gossip, which she then passed on to the Confederates. The aged General Winfield Scott's meticulous military secretary, Colonel E. D. Keyes, confessed that the blandishments of such ladies from the slave states often lured him "to the brink of the precipice."

General Scott, General-in-Chief of the Army, was old for his position. As a native-born Virginian, for years he had been promoting promising Southerners to choice military ranks. The best of these officers now ungratefully accepted Confederate commands, leaving the bewildered old man with rapidly promoted, inexperienced officers to command his own raw troops.

Living under wartime conditions in the White House was a trial to Mary's guests, as Cousin Elizabeth Grimsley soon found. Secretary Seward gave an elegant dinner party on May 9, following a matinee performance given by the 71st New York Regiment, Dodworth's Band. Mary had attended the matinee with Lincoln and the boys, while Elizabeth Grimsley and White House Secretary John Hay represented the First Family at the magnificent Seward dinner. Afterwards they were unable to re-enter the White House because Hay had neglected to find out the evening's special password. They encountered much red tape before they rejoined the First Family.

The President, believing that a change from their "militarized home" and the continuous criticism might be good for his wife, suggested she take Elizabeth on a brief trip to New York. As the railroads were now interrupted by wartime conditions, the two women took a steamer to Perth Amboy, from where they con-

A Rose for Mrs. Lincoln : : page 110

tinued to their destination by train. The weather being fine, they took a sightseeing drive by open carriage through Brooklyn's Greenwood Cemetery, then a great point of interest with its wide roads, splendid landscaping and fantastic monuments. Somewhat miffed, newspaper reporters did not hear of the New York visit until after the distinguished ladies had left the city next day. Back in Washington, the First Lady and her cousin were horrified to read press accounts of their large expenditures at Lord and Taylor, and other leading stores. Mary had supposedly bought a point lace shawl for three thousand dollars, and Elizabeth had "bought" another for a thousand. ". . . and par parenthesis," quips Elizabeth, "this was the nearest I ever came to having one." In truth, neither of the women had done any shopping at all.

Their next visit to New York was more of an official nature for, in spite of the war, Congress had appropriated $20,000 to refurnish the Executive Mansion. Never before in her life had Mrs. Lincoln possessed so much money to spend as she pleased. This time they were harassed by reporters at every carriage stop.

Elizabeth makes the interesting observation,

> When the First Lady bought the dinner set for the
> Executive Mansion, she ordered a set made for herself, with
> her initial, and this latter, I know, was not paid for by the
> district commissioner, as was most unkindly charged when
> it was stored away. Unfortunately, too, many presents were
> sent marked "personal gifts," and were accepted, but Mr.
> Lincoln was not in this respect "worldly wise" and Mrs.
> Lincoln could not anticipate the storm of censure which
> fell upon her.

They enjoyed selecting new carpets and furniture for the large north room, where "the best in the family suite was most shabby." The most handsome thing in it was a French mahogany bedstead that was split from top to bottom. It "looked as if it had survived many Presidents and worn out the patience of many servants trying to keep it in reputable order."

After much careful thought the First Lady chose a solferino

and gold dinner service for the White House, patriotically designed with an eagle emblazoned in the center. The edges were rimmed with plain maroon. She ordered handsome mantel ornaments and vases for the Blue and Green Rooms, and a 700-piece set of Bohemian cut glass. Socially prominent Mary Clemmer Ames, the writer, never an ardent admirer of the First Lady, even complimented Mary on one of the carpets.

> The most exquisite carpet ever on the East Room was a velvet one chosen by Mrs. Lincoln. Its ground was of pale sea green, and in effect it looked as if ocean, in gleaming and transparent waves, were tossing roses at your feet.

In spite of a war, Mary was determined to have the President's House furnished in the latest style and best quality. As *The White House—An Historic Guide* compiled during the tenure of Jacqueline Kennedy as First Lady, notes some hundred years later,

> Some of the many things she ordered are now in the Lincoln Bedroom. The carved chair in the Treaty Room, recently recovered from storage, was probably acquired at this time. Indeed, it is very similar to the chair in which Lincoln is seated in the Healy portrait.

Until the weather became too warm, the President and First Lady kept up their Saturday afternoon receptions. At such times the Mall was a fashionable place for the promenaders, with the Marine Band supplying the music. The First Family usually received on the South Balcony all those who chose to join them. This was surprising, considering the many threats received through the mail. Their view from the balcony was still a dismal one, for the Washington Monument in its unfinished state was made all the more desolate by the weeds and rubbish. Even so, an enterprising photographer had seen fit to set up his camera there, of which Cousin Elizabeth notes this fascinating tidbit, "I think his were the first *cartes de visites* taken, at least in Washington, and the photograph album came into vogue."

A Rose for Mrs. Lincoln : : *page 112*

On June 3, Mary personally saw that the White House was draped in mourning for Senator Douglas, her old friend, and Abraham's rival. Of necessity the show of mourning was brief for the President had arranged to give a dinner for members of the Diplomatic Corps, which according to the Washington *Star* of June 7, 1861, was "in many respects, the most brilliant affair of the sort that has ever taken place in the Executive Mansion."

The First Lady found herself praised instead of condemned, as she usually was. The press story continued,

> Through the good taste of Mrs. Lincoln, the stiff, artificial flowers heretofore ornamenting the Presidential tables were wholly discarded and their places delightfully supplied by fragrant, natural flowers. The blue room was decorated with cut flowers; and the chandeliers gracefully festooned with wreaths and flowers, indeed the senses of sight and smell were delighted at every turn by beautiful and fragrant pyramids and wreaths from the floral riches of the White House conservatories and grounds. The dinner was served in a style to indicate that Mrs. Lincoln's good taste and good judgment had exercised supervision in this department also.

Mary spoke French with the Chilean Ambassador and his wife, neither of whom knew any English. Elizabeth speaks of "the exchange of civilities in the tendering of elaborate snuff-boxes, not only among the diplomats, but all the ladies."

Yet, in spite of official entertainments, the grim business of war continued. On June 10 the Federals suffered defeat at Big Bethel, Virginia, followed by that fateful Sunday, July 21, which Elizabeth calls "the most memorable day ever known in Washington since it was captured by the British army, in the last war." At midnight the streets of the capital echoed as troops marched toward the Potomac, urged on by cheering crowds bidding them "On to Richmond and Victory." Early next morning the roar of artillery at Bull Run rumbled through the sultry air. Hundreds of curious Washington residents commandeered every available conveyance to take them within watching distance of the battlefield. General Scott was on hand to open all dispatches, read them, announce their contents, and then give his orders, all in the presence of the excited throng.

The First Lady and her cousin waited eagerly for news of the battle, which at first was good. "Bull Run, the key of the enemy's position, had been taken, and the enemy completely routed." Their relief was short-lived for further dispatches brought news of Bull Run's recapture, with terrific loss of life to both sides.

Both in the White House and in the streets outside rumors spread fast that the Confederates were advancing on Washington, that the city would be shelled and captured. Alexandria and Baltimore would join the Confederates, it was feared, for the regiments keeping them in subjection had been removed. "It was a time of intense anxiety," says Elizabeth. "And can you wonder at it?"

Even so, notes Elizabeth, there was a wedding "that beautiful Sabbath evening" in Dr. Phineas D. Gurley's Presbyterian church on New York Avenue, when his daughter was married to a young officer "amid flowers, music and light." Afterwards the bridegroom left to join his regiment. Bayonets glistened in the moonlight, and army wagons rolled by to fetch the wounded as the White House ladies returned home from that "sad church wedding."

Then a telegram from General Scott was delivered to the President: "The day is lost! Save Washington and the remnant of the army." At 2 A.M., a special army correspondent arrived with news that a body of New Jersey soldiers had arrested the flight of the demoralized fugitive troops. Eleven thousand men not in the Centerville fight had made a brave stand with a battery against the enemy's advance. This brought temporary relief. General Scott, upon arriving at the White House, first insisted that the First Lady, her children, and Elizabeth go to bed. Although they obeyed, they found little sleep, for through a heavy rain they could hear the muffled grind of horse-drawn ambulances bearing the wounded to hospitals, offset by the steady tramp of men marching to the front.

Next day it was still raining, the downpour lasting for thirty-six hours. The weather did not prevent the President or his wife from visiting the wounded. When General Scott insisted that Mrs. Lincoln, Elizabeth, and the children be sent North to safety, Mary looked at her husband and asked, "Will you go with us?"

"Most assuredly I will not leave at this juncture," he replied.

"Then I will not leave you at this juncture," was her firm answer.

Try as he would, the General could not get the First Lady to change her mind. Finally, in desperation he suggested that Elizabeth should leave with Willie and Tad. Again he met with defeat. Elizabeth wrote, "Nor was this the only occasion when it was thought best for her [the First Lady] to leave the Capitol for a place of safety, but always with like results."

The Federals, under General Irvin McDowell, were defeated by the Confederates, under Generals Joseph Eggleston Johnston and Pierre Gustave Toutant Beauregard. The South's success at Bull Run encouraged them to continue the war. President Lincoln issued a call for 300,000 more troops, getting a speedy and enthusiastic response. "Rally Round the Flag" became their stirring war song.

CHAPTER TWELVE

THE REPUBLICAN QUEEN

The Republican Queen, as her enemies dubbed her, commenced the winter levees early, telling her private secretary, the understanding William Stoddard, that she was still willing to do her duty "while my smiling guests pull me in pieces."

It was December, a good time to show off all the splendor of the newly-transformed White House. Bravely she faced her detractors in a gown of figured silk brocade, her head wreathed with flowers. During her first year as First Lady she had been the unwelcome recipient of more personal publicity in the Northern press than the President himself. Most of it was unfavorable. So persistent had been the malicious rumors of her treason that the Senate members of the Committee on the Conduct of the War even gathered in secret session to consider them. They were startled and ashamed when the President appeared unannounced to state formally that no member of his family was holding treasonable communication with the enemy. The inquisitors shifted uncomfortably in their seats, then quickly dropped the subject.

As the guests moved from room to room there were exclamations of delight at what they saw. The old furniture was freshly varnished so that it even smelled clean. The chairs and sofas had been upholstered in crimson satin brocatelle, tufted and laid in folds on the backs, "rendering a modern appearance."

The East Room had been done over with a heavy cloth velvet paper in the Parisian style so beloved by Mrs. Lincoln, with a striking pattern of garnet, crimson, and gold. It was regally offset by the new "all in one piece" carpet made in Glasgow, with designs of wreaths, bouquets, fruit, flowers, and graceful vases. Over white needle-wrought lace inner curtains, imported from Switzerland, hung draperies of French crimson brocatelle trimmed with golden fringes and tassels, framed by glittering gilt cornices.

The Blue Room looked gay with new carpet and paper; while the Green Room had been completely renovated. Only the famed historic painting of George Washington, saved in the War of 1812 by Dolley Madison, remained of the old Red Room accessories. The State Bedroom had been royally papered light purple in a most un-Republican fashion. Cushioned and canopied in rich purple figured satin, trimmed with gold lace, the enormous bed was fit for a king. Even the Lincolns' private apartments had been considerably brightened by the addition of some modern furniture; the Executive Chamber was also freshly wallpapered. The *Herald* correspondent did not approve of the well-worn desks and chairs that remained in the President's office, calling them "too rickety to venerate," though N. P. Willis, publisher of the popular *Home Journal* magazine, noted benevolently that "Mr. Lincoln don't complain." A large rack to hold war maps, of which the President was very proud, stood out as the only piece of new furniture.

The President did not understand the high cost of the luxurious items purchased for the White House, in much the same way as he was unaware that his wife was using her credit as First Lady to run up large dress bills. He was not told until she exceeded the Congressional appropriation for refurnishing the Mansion. After all the monies had been spent there was still some $7,000 owing to a Philadelphia decorator named Carryl who was now pressing for payment. Half of this had been spent on the gorgeous wallpaper, to purchase which the man had even made a trip to Paris. Over eight hundred dollars had gone upon wallpapering alone for the East Room. Scraping the walls of the President's Room, then papering them and supplying gilt moldings cost more than four hundred dollars! The President was shocked at such expenditure, declaring he would pay the outstanding bill from his own pocket. In desperation Mrs. Lincoln sent for Major B. B. French, Commissioner of Public Buildings to help her.

Major French, who presented important guests to the First

Lady at official receptions, was a stout, choleric old man with curling gray side-whiskers, brushed towards the front. When, in her feminine Southern way, she flattered him, the major eyed her suspiciously. However, he was patient and kind to her, although at times her spendthrift ways made him wince. In this instance Major French answered her call at nine in the morning, when she appeared before him in a wrapper, to promise tearfully that in future she would tell her husband it was "common to over-run appropriations."

The bewhiskered major melted before her tears. Without involving Mrs. Lincoln further, he told the President that the Philadelphia decorator had presented a bill much in excess of the appropriation. He now needed the President's approval before he could ask for the extra money.

"It can never have my approval," grumbled Lincoln. "I'll pay it out of my own pocket first. It would stink in the nostrils of the American people to have it said that the President of the United States had approved a bill over-running an appropriation of $20,000 for flub dubs for this damned old house, when the soldiers cannot have blankets."

Then he demanded to know who had employed Carryl in the first place. Major French declared ignorance of the matter, saying that maybe Lincoln's private secretary, Nicolay, knew. The private secretary was called in. "How did this man Carryl get into this house?" demanded the President.

"I do not know, sir," was the reply.

"Who employed him?"

"Mrs. Lincoln, I suppose."

"Yes," said the President resignedly. "Mrs. Lincoln—well, I suppose Mrs. Lincoln *must* bear the blame, let her bear it, I swear I won't!"

Nicolay was ordered to fetch Carryl's account, which the President proceeded to read. " 'Elegant, grand carpet, $2,500.' I should like to know where a carpet worth $2,500 can be put," he complained. Major French suggested that it might be in the East Room, but he would have done well to have kept quiet. "No," snapped the President, "that cost $10,000, a monstrous extravigance [*sic*—French's own spelling]." It was wicked to spend one cent at such a time, the President insisted, saying, "The house was furnished well enough, better than any one we ever lived in. . . ." Then declaring he was so overwhelmed with other business that he could not attend to everything, the President began to pace the floor.

In fairness to the First Lady, French was not altogether honest with the President. He was perfectly aware that his predecessor, W. S. Wood had authorized the purchase of the expensive wallpaper, charging it to an annual allowance of six thousand dollars, disbursed by the Commissioner of Public Buildings for repairs on the Executive Mansion. The money had actually been spent painting the White House exterior and for necessary repairs, but French did not want to be blamed for Wood's mistakes. Upon succeeding Wood, French had told Carryl that there were no funds to meet his bill. Vainly he had tried to talk the extravagant First Lady out of papering the rooms, begging her to wait until the following year. Finally, he managed to get the wallpaper costs included in a convenient appropriation for sundry civil expenses. This presumably covered the cost of the "elegant grand carpet" which had annoyed Lincoln so much.

The First Lady had sorely taxed Major French upon this occasion, yet although he continued to call her "a curiosity" he admired the way she fended off the false stories circulated about her.

CHAPTER THIRTEEN

CRITICS AND THE FAMILY

The year wore on, every day bringing more criticism of the unfortunate First Lady. The disgusting insinuations concerning her loyalty and antecedents preyed upon her mind, causing her sick headaches to increase in frequency. Albert Shaw quotes some of the charges made against Mary Todd Lincoln.

> The extreme antislavery elements, and these became increasingly large, grew deeply suspicious because Mrs. Lincoln had come from Kentucky. It was enough for the censorious fanatics that her own brothers and other relatives were living in the South and were serving in the Confederate Army. Some people have believed until this day that Mrs. Lincoln was a Southern spy in the White House. The extreme elements in the South, on the other hand, hated Mrs. Lincoln because, in point of fact, she was intensely loyal to her husband and to the Union cause, although of Southern origin. People in the back districts of all the Southern states were told that Mrs. Lincoln had Negro blood in her veins and was profligate in her personal life.
>
> . . . .
>
> Mary Todd, Lincoln's wife, had been more unpleasantly criticized from various standpoints private and public than any other woman in the long succession of Mistresses of the White House. . . . Far more intense and more penetrating, however, was the sectional prejudice due

to the cleavage between North and South. The nation's capital city—always a hotbed of malicious gossip—was dominated in the social sense by Southern sympathizers. The District of Columbia, wedged in between Virginia and Maryland, was sullenly hostile to the idea of having the Lincoln family in the White House.

The sheer loneliness of her intolerable position made Mary extremely possessive of the President, and she was scarcely able to conceal her jealousy in public when other women flattered him. "Mother, I insist that I must talk with somebody," he reasoned. "I can't stand around like a simpleton and say nothing." When she tried to strike the names of Secretary of the Treasury Salmon Chase and his beautiful daughter from her dinner list because they displeased her, the President quietly had them restored.

At times when she could scarcely bear the pain of her headaches, she would argue loudly with her husband, afterwards complaining, "Sometimes . . . being worn down, he spoke crabbedly."

She had always been outspoken and opinionated, even as a child, but never like this, even trying to interfere in the conduct of the war. She detested McClellan, calling him a "humbug," and urged her husband to replace him. A general to meet the genius of the South's own Robert E. Lee needed to be found. Visiting New York, Mary wrote the President that "many say they would almost worship you if you would put a fighting general in the place of McClellan." Finally the President did remove McClellan, not because of pressure from his wife, but because he failed to follow up the advantage gained by his first victory at Antietam. His replacement was Ulysses S. Grant, destined to become one of the great American military figures and a future President of the United States. Mary also detested Grant, calling him a "butcher" because he had "no regard for life." The President did not listen, although he did once tell her, "Suppose that we give you command of the army. No doubt you would do much better than any general that has been tried."

"Her personal antipathies are quick and strong, and at times they find hasty and resentful forms of expression," said Secretary Stoddard of the First Lady, who said of herself, "My husband placed great confidence in my knowledge of human nature, he had not much knowledge of men." She constantly reminded him of the hypocrisy with which he was surrounded. "You are too suspicious," he answered. "I give you credit for sagacity, but you are disposed to magnify trifles." Unscrupulous politicians and would-be officeholders sent the First Lady presents such as a carriage and other expensive gifts which she unwisely accepted. Later, when they asked her to intercede upon their behalf for some political appointment, she was hard put to refuse them. When a man complained that the First Lady was interfering in political affairs and influencing her husband, the President replied, "I myself manage all important matters. In little things I have got along through life by letting my wife run her end of the machine pretty much in her own way."

Cousin Elizabeth Grimsley records the following concerning a minor appointment.

> Mrs. Lincoln and I took the President by storm, one morning, with the demand for an appointment, which so surprised him that he could only hold up his hands and exclaim "Et tu Brute." Our persistence became so great that surprise was changed to laughter, amid which he said: "Well! but you have not told me what you want, or the merits of the case."
>
> Nothing less than the consulship at Dundee for our old Scotch Minister of Springfield, the Rev. Dr. James Smith, to whom we were all very much attached. An intellectual, powerful man, a perfect "Boanerges," who could thunder out "the terrors of the law" as well as proclaim the love of the Gospel, but who had passed the line, and given way to a younger man.
>
> Mr. Lincoln hesitated: "He who hesitates is lost"; we pressed the matter. "The old Doctor was a warm personal friend, had been with us in joy and sorrow, was well-fitted for the post, which was one not much in demand, was an ardent Republican, and he wanted to spend his last days on his 'native heather'," and many words to like effect.

He rose, laughing and said "You know Clarissa married Peter to get rid of him, send your preacher to the Cabinet Room," from whence he emerged a happy man, and Mr. Lincoln well pleased that he could confer the consulship on him. But he exacted a promise from us that it should be the last time we would "corner" him. My private opinion is he had already settled the whole thing in his own mind but wanted to see the extent of our interest in this old friend.

The First Lady recorded that "Mr. Lincoln was mild in his manners, but he was a terribly firm man when he set his foot down. None of us, no man or woman, could rule him after he had once fully made up his mind."

As the war progressed the President received many requests for appeals and pardons. According to Elizabeth, these were "often pathetic, moving Mr. Lincoln's kindly heart unspeakably." He gave orders that none who had such an appeal to present should be turned away without his giving the case a personal hearing. "Some of my generals complain that I impair discipline and subordination, but it makes me feel rested after a hard day's work, if I can find some good excuse to save a man's life," he once said. Added to the appeals of worried relatives were those of his small son Tad, himself afflicted with a cleft palate. "Think Faver," he would beg, "if it was your own little boy who was just tired after fighting, and marching all day, that he could not keep awake, much as he tried to."

Some of these cries for mercy took place in the family apartments, where Tad, abetted by his sensitive mother, only increased the strain on everybody. Gently but firmly, the President shut his loved ones out of the room. The First Lady's heart was equally tender. When she heard that a young soldier, William Scott, was to be shot for falling asleep on picket duty she "grew so nervous" that the President actually told General McClellan that "the Lady President" greatly hoped the man would be pardoned. He was.

When the time came for Elizabeth to return home, Mary and Robert accompanied her to Niagara Falls, where Elizabeth's cousin General Charles F. Smith was on hand to escort her for the rest

Abraham Lincoln. *From the collections of the Library of Congress.*

of her journey. Elizabeth was sorry to go, for in addition to having been close to Mary, during her White House stay she had come to know and appreciate the real Abraham Lincoln.

Elizabeth best explains her feelings at parting.

> It was a sad parting with Mr. Lincoln. A strong attachment had sprung up between him and myself, as a six months intimacy, under such trying circumstances had developed unsuspected qualities in both of us. I had, from a child, known him, he was intimate and a valued kinsman in my father's family. I had been much with my cousin Mary, in our girlhood, was one of the bridesmaids, saw the ring bearing the motto, "Love is eternal," placed upon her finger, and always a welcomed guest in their home, yet so reticent was Mr. Lincoln, so deferential to ladies, so introspective, if I may use that word, that when I was thrown closely with him in his family relations, I felt as if I had been almost a stranger to his true character. I could readily understand how his wife, the constant recipient and witness of his many characteristics and tenderness, should have been so devoted to him. I can not feel as if it were a betrayal of hospitality to speak thus of the inner life of a household, of which I had been so long a favored guest, and under such circumstances which threw personal traits into strong prominence.

"God bless you, my cousin," were the President's parting words. Afterwards she recalled them as a benediction.

After parting from Elizabeth, the First Lady felt in need of a change. Tired, she took a holiday at the seaside, where the New York *Herald* reported that she was going to "enjoy the purer air and more healthful breezes of Long Branch." The resort's young ladies were longing to meet Robert, who, according to the *Herald*, seems to have been something of a disappointment:

> He does everything very well, but avoids doing anything extraordinary. He doesn't talk much; he doesn't dance differently. . . . In short, he is only Mr. Robert Lincoln.

... He does nothing whatever to attract attention and shows by every gentlemanly way how much he dislikes this fulsome sort of admiration, but it comes, all the same. ... Mr. Robert is happier when smoking a pipe, student fashion, and doing his share in a good laugh than among all the doings of the Branch.

At home in the White House, Willie was proving to be especially studious, with a literary taste. Upon the death of Colonel Edward Baker, the family friend for whom the baby Eddie Lincoln had been named, Willie had written a poem, sending it to the Editor of the *National Republican*, with the following brief note.

Washington, D.C.
October 30, 1861.

Dear Sir:—
  I enclose you my first attempt at poetry.
        Yours truly,
                WM. W. LINCOLN.

LINES ON THE DEATH OF COLONEL EDWARD BAKER

There was no patriot like Baker,
So noble and so true;
He fell as a soldier on the field,
His face to the sky of blue

His voice is silent in the hall
Which oft his presence graced;
No more he'll hear the loud acclaim
Which rang from place to place.

No squeamish notions filled his breast,
The Union was his theme;
'No surrender and no compromise,'
His day-thought and night's dream.

A Rose for Mrs. Lincoln : : *page 126*

> His Country has *her* part to pay
> To'rds those he has left behind;
> His widow and his children all,
> She must always keep in mind.

Reading over the lines written by her ten-year-old son, the First Lady began to tremble, wanting to weep and yet not being able to.

She went out into the garden and there, among the trees that were already losing their golden leaves, she found Willie and Tad, happily playing together.

CHAPTER FOURTEEN

WILLIE

The President's wife made her first public appearance that winter at a White House reception held New Year's Day, 1862, shortly followed by a brilliant levee. The day following the levee, Mrs. Keckley went to the White House to fit Mrs. Lincoln for a new dress. The First Lady seemed deep in thought.

"'Lizabeth," she began, "I have an idea. These are war times and we must be as economical as possible. You know the President is expected to give a series of state dinners every winter, and these dinners are very costly; now I want to avoid this expense; and my idea is, that if I give three large receptions, the state dinners can be scratched from the program. What do you think, 'Lizabeth?"

Mrs. Keckley thought that the President's wife was right, although the President was not so sure. "Mother," he said, shaking his head, "I am afraid your plan will not work."

"But it *will* work," she insisted, "if you will only determine that it *shall* work."

The President was not convinced. It would only result in more criticism, for the public hated breaking established customs. However, Mrs. Lincoln finally won her point, and engraved invitation cards were issued during January for the first reception to be held the next month.

Although the President was paying for the affair out of his own pocket, it was as he had feared—the newspapers had a field day condemning in advance "My Lady President's Ball." Five hundred invitations were issued; the uninvited immediately assailed Mrs. Lincoln. In the end she placated all she could by sending out more invitations, even to the representatives of her most unfavorable press.

Abolitionists who had helped the Lincolns into the White House with their support now openly criticized what they termed "merrymaking" at the White House. Senator Benjamin F. Wade of Ohio expressed his regrets. "Are the President and Mrs. Lincoln aware that there is a civil war? If they are not, Mr. and Mrs. Wade are, and for that reason decline to participate in feasting and dancing."

A series of well-timed editorials in the New York *Herald* "defended" the President's wife in such a way as to do her more harm than good. She had, they said, a double motive for giving the grand soirée. The first was to show the "haughty secessionist dames" in Washington who had closed their houses and refused to go out, that there still remained a fashionable society among the loyal residents. The second, insisted the *Herald*, was her limiting of the guests in order to "weed the Presidential mansion" of "the long-haired, white-coated, tobacco-chewing and expectorant abolitionist" politicians. Said the *Herald* with mock concern, "Mrs. Lincoln is responsible to Congress for the Presidential spoons, and it is not safe to trust an ice cream thus manipulated in the itching fingers of these sweet smelling patriots." The First Lady was accused of having intentionally insulted the powerful and revengeful radical faction of the Republicans.

Other newspapers carried advance stories and discussions on "Mrs. Lincoln's Party"; a weekly publication printed an entire column of mournful verses, entitled "My Lady President's Ball," supposed to be sung by a wounded volunteer in the hospital!

While final preparations for the party were being made, Willie took sick with a severe cold and fever. Tad also had a cold. It was believed they had caught them while riding a pony given them by a family friend. The First Lady sent for Mrs. Keckley to help nurse her sons; she noted that Willie "when able to walk was almost constantly by his mother's side." When Willie's fever grew worse, his worried mother, remembering little Eddie's death, determined to postpone the controversial reception. After all the trouble there had been over the party, the President thought that the invitations should not be withdrawn until Willie's doctor was consulted.

The doctor was reassuring. Willie was somewhat better, he told them; there was every reason for an early recovery. The boy, he insisted, faced no immediate danger; the party could go on as planned. The Lincolns took the doctor's advice, but on the evening of the reception, Willie's condition showed a decided turn for the worse. His mother, much distressed, sat by the boy's bed, holding his hand. The doctor was summoned and, even though Willie's breathing was labored, again insisted there was no cause for alarm.

Mrs. Keckley managed to calm the First Lady sufficiently to arrange her hair. Then she helped her dress in a half-mourning ensemble worn out of respect for Albert, the English Prince Consort who had died of typhoid fever the previous December. Tales of the hysterical screams of the widowed Queen Victoria echoing through the ghostly corridors of Windsor Castle had deeply impressed the First Lady.

The gown of white satin worn by Mrs. Lincoln was lavishly flounced with black lace, and was cut low in the latest fashion, bunches of crepe myrtle gracing her bosom. Her Parisian headdress was complemented with no other ornaments but pearls.

The President was standing, hands behind him, with his back to the fire, when his wife swept in. Seeing her ample train he remarked, "Whew! our cat has a long tail to-night." When she did not reply, he continued: "Mother, it is my opinion, if some of that tail was nearer the head, it would be in better style." She adopted a look of offended dignity, then taking his arm, descended the stairs to their guests. Mrs. Keckley, left alone with the sick child, recalled how "the rich notes of the Marine Band in the apartments below came to the sick-room in soft, subdued murmurs, like the wild, faint sobbing of far-off spirits."

The much-maligned party was a social triumph for the First Lady. Not content with local caterers, she had engaged Maillard of New York to prepare the supper. Some days previously, he had arrived with a retinue of cooks, waiters, and artists in confectionery.

A Rose for Mrs. Lincoln : : page 130

She stood with the President in the center of the flower-decked East Room. A goodly showing of the Diplomatic Corps made a splash of brilliance in the Blue Room, where their cosmopolitan chatter delighted Mrs. Lincoln.

Distinguished citizens mingled with Cabinet members and senators. The French princes were there, and so was Prince Felix Salm-Salm, a Prussian cavalry officer serving on General Louis Blenker's staff. In evidence too were a number of the First Lady's enemies, including Miss Kate Chase, daughter of the Secretary of the Treasury. This young lady had infuriated Mrs. Lincoln by holding court at White House levees.

At eleven o'clock Mrs. Lincoln promenaded around the East Room, leaning upon the President's arm. He had vetoed any dancing because of the war, although Bob and other young people were present.

At suppertime it was discovered, to the hostess's consternation, that a servant had misplaced the State Dining Room key. "I am in favor of a forward movement," suggested one guest. "An advance to the front is only retarded by the imbecility of commanders," said another, mimicking a recent Congressional speech. General McClellan, struggling as hard as anybody else in the throng, laughed at the "insult."

The key was found at last, the impatient guests swarmed in, to be met by the sight of Maillard's remarkable inspirations. There were hives swarming with lifelike bees and filled with *charlotte russe*; a fountain graced by nougat water-nymphs stood close to a spun sugar helmet topped with waving plumes. A sugar Fort Pickens rose from a side table, surmounted by candy birds; the frigate *Union*, with forty guns and all sails set, was supported by cherubs draped in the Stars and Stripes.

Several times that evening the Lincolns visited their sick child upstairs. When greeting General John C. Frémont, the President spoke of Willie's illness. Mrs. Keckley noted "the sadness that rested upon the face of Mrs. Lincoln," and of how "the night passed slowly; morning came, and Willie was worse."

She stayed on to help with the nursing. Tad's cold improved, but Willie developed typhoid fever. Mrs. Lincoln scarcely left his side, though there were those who even then accused her of heartlessness, saying that the White House was filled with music and laughter while her little son lay dying.

Mrs. Keckley, worn out with watching, was not in the room when Willie died, but was sent for immediately. The mother went into such convulsions of grief that those present feared for her sanity. Says Mrs. Keckley,

> The President kindly bent over his wife, took her by the arm and gently led her to the window. With a stately, solemn gesture, he pointed to the lunatic asylum.
> "Mother, do you see that large white building on the hill yonder? Try and control your grief, or it will drive you mad, and we may have to send you there."

But Mary Lincoln's grief could not be assuaged, so they led her to bed and pulled down the blinds. Visitors paying their respects below shuddered at the sound of her hysterical weeping. She could not attend the funeral, just as she had been unable to attend baby Eddie's in Springfield. Something devoured her strength and snapped her self-control. Clinging to Mrs. Keckley, with whom she felt a bond—the dressmaker having recently lost a son fighting for the Union in Missouri—she begged only for the bunch of flowers that Willie clasped in his coffin.

The President was bowed with grief, going often to the window as if half expecting to see Willie at play. "I know that he is much better off in heaven," he said to Mrs. Keckley, "but then we loved him so . . ."

Willie's body was temporarily laid to rest in the receiving vault of a Washington cemetery, ready to be taken back to Springfield when the family returned. For weeks the First Lady refused to have removed the black crepe which had been hung all over the White House. She could not bear to look at Willie's picture, or ever again enter either the room where he died or the Green Room in which his small body was embalmed. Months later she still could not restrain her outbursts of grief. In this she was not alone, for even the President repeatedly gave way to uncontrollable expressions of sorrow. The First Lady confided to her half-sister Emilie Helm, "If I had not felt the spur of necessity urging me to cheer Mr. Lincoln, whose grief was as great as my own, I could never have smiled again."

There was still no rest from the cruel tongues of men. Now the radical politicians accused the bereaved First Lady of having given the text of a Presidential Message to the Chevalier Wikoff, who passed it on to the eager press of the New York *Herald*. Later Wikoff confessed that the White House head gardener, John Watt, and not the First Lady, had been his informant. This Wikoff, a cosmopolitan and well-traveled man, was usually called the "Chevalier" Wikoff because of a decoration bestowed upon him by Queen Isabella of Spain. He had been planted in the White House as a social spy by the New York *Herald*.

His compliments about the First Lady's dress appealed to her vanity. How could she be other than flattered when the New York *Herald* declared, "This Kentucky girl, this Western matron, this Republican Queen, puts to the blush and entirely eclipses the first ladies of Europe—the excellent Victoria, the pensive Eugénie and the brilliant Isabella."

Such accusations as that resulting from the ignominious behavior of Wikoff, a man she had trusted, hurt and bewildered the First Lady. She turned to expensive mourning gowns for consolation, buying black jet jewelry to match. Now only the finest straw bonnets and the sheerest crepe veiling pleased her. She ordered sets of collars and undersleeves for her rich black dresses. Her credit was already being questioned. "I have your money ready for you," she wrote boldly across one order.

The President tried to humor his wife, yet his complete disregard for personal safety was no consolation to a woman who clung to him whenever he left the White House on his own, begging him to take care. Much to the consternation of his bodyguards, he loved nothing better than to stride freely among the crowds in the streets, a shawl around his shoulders in cold weather. This was how Vinnie Ream, a young post office worker, fresh in Washington from Fort Smith, Arkansas, first set eyes upon him. She was deeply touched "by the lines of sadness on his face."

At times Mary was not overly cautious for her own safety either, especially when the curious with little effort could invade the family quarters. Even Mrs. Greenhow, with whose little girl,

Rose, Tad and Willie played, had been arrested as a Confederate spy. Truly her mother's daughter, Little Rose—as she was familiarly called—climbed a tree in the garden, from which she shouted, "Mother has been arrested!" Before she was pulled down from her perch she had successfully frightened off several Confederate callers.

On a wintry January evening, the Greenhows were taken through gaslit streets to the Old Capitol, now a military prison. Twelve years previously, when it was a boarding house, Mrs. Greenhow had ministered there to her dying idol, the South Carolina statesman, John C. Calhoun. Now she returned a prisoner and, with regal dignity, compared herself to the ill-fated Marie Antoinette. Little Rose provoked the guards with a warning: "You have got one of the hardest little rebels here that you ever saw."

Later, Mrs. Greenhow's own home became a women's prison with herself an inmate. It was relief to leave the Old Capitol where she had been allowed no privacy at all. Visitors to Washington called her new prison "Fort Greenhow," and soon it became a tourist attraction.

Prohibiting the use of flowers inside the White House because Willie had loved them, the First Lady next banned the popular Marine Band concerts which the public so enjoyed, because she could no longer bear happy music. This loss of public pleasure was most unpopular; the press grumbled that mothers across the nation were losing sons in battle; why was her grief any different from theirs?

Shopping was Mrs. Lincoln's only solace. The purchase of expensive mourning became even more of an obsession; as to its cost she was utterly oblivious. To one firm she wrote:

> I want you to select me the *very finest* and blackest and lightest long crepe veil, and bordered as they bring them. Please get me the finest that can be obtained. Want a *very, very* fine black crepe veil, round corners and folds around. Want one of very fine black silk net—with folds around for summer—round at corners and short. . . . I liked the undersleeves and collars. Please have me *two more*, white and black collars mixed, with cuffs to match. . . .

I want the genteelest and tastiest you can find and have made.

But even the finest mourning did not bring Willie back. She turned her energies to visiting the wounded, which proved to be a welcome and successful therapy. When a case of expensive wine and rum was given to the White House, the First Lady exclaimed, "They do not seem to have forgotten anything, but what shall I do with it? Mr. Lincoln never touches any strong drink. I never use it. I will thank these gentlemen, and the poor soldiers shall have it all." She gave it to be used for medicinal purposes.

Now she was seen many times a week at the hospitals accompanied by attendants carrying baskets of dainties prepared under her own supervision at the White House, and bunches of flowers to cheer the makeshift wards. She organized the distribution of more fresh fruit to the military hospitals, and the Washington *Republican* insisted that she had contributed more from her private purse to aid the wounded soldiers, than any other woman in Washington. Then there were letters to write for the dying. She spared herself nothing. Years later Frank G. Thompson, an old soldier, wrote nostalgically of Mary Lincoln, "She lives in the memory of those whose agonies she soothed with loving words."

While Southerners satirized her as "the Yankee nurse," the Northern critics were somewhat kinder, for they could hardly find fault in a woman who gave so much of her time to the sick. The President was pleased with the First Lady's efforts, personally writing such notes as the following to help her:

> Executive Mansion,
> Washington.
> August 16, 1862.
>
> Hon. Hiram Barney,
> New York.
>
> Mrs. L. has $1000 for the benefit of the hospitals, and she will be obliged and send the pay if you will be so good as to select and send her $200 worth of good lemons and $100 worth of good oranges.
>
> A. LINCOLN.

Willie :: page 135

On November 29, 1862, when Mrs. Lincoln returned from a visit North, the Washington *Chronicle* declared, "The sick and wounded soldiers in our hospitals will hail her return with joy."

The President, as a diversion, persuaded his wife to invite the young opera singer, Adelina Maria Clorinda Patti to the White House, having heard her sing in 1853 when she was only ten years old. In 1861 she had played Amina in *La Sonnambula* with much success. Patti says of her visit,

> The following afternoon my manager took me to the White House and we were received by Mrs. Lincoln in one of the big parlors. The President's wife was a handsome woman, almost regal in her deep black and expansive crinoline, only an outline of white at throat and wrists. Her manner was most gracious without a particle of reserve or stiffness. "My dear, it is very kind of you to come to see us," she said. Taking both my hands in hers and smiling in my face, she added, "I have wanted to see you;—to see the young girl who has done so much, who has set the whole world talking of her wonderful singing."

Then Patti sang "The Last Rose of Summer" which caused the First Lady to weep. At the President's request she rendered "Home Sweet Home," then, also in tears, she took leave of the bereaved parents.

The Lincolns spent the summer in the Anderson Cottage, which was part of the Soldiers' Home that stood on a wooded hill three miles beyond the city boundary. It had been founded with part of the tribute money levied by General Scott upon Mexico City, and was used as a kind of "Summer White House." Although absent herself, the First Lady still forbade the White House Marine Concerts, causing the Secretary of the Navy, Gideon Welles, to tell the President how much the people missed them. When Mrs. Lincoln still would not change her mind, military concerts were diplomatically given twice weekly in nearby Lafayette Square.

Even months after Willie's death, when public receptions were again resumed, the First Lady swathed herself from head to foot in heavy mourning. She did give a private reception to honor the famed midget, General Tom Thumb and his bride, the former Lavinia Warren, whom he had recently married in Grace Church, New York City. Cabinet members attended the reception to meet the minute couple. However, even though they had been caressed by the crowned heads of Europe, there was one member of Mrs. Lincoln's family who was not enthused at the opportunity. This was young Robert, who refused to be present at the reception.

Mrs. Lincoln's next levee, according to Major French, was such a "crusher" that the First Lady saw fit to remark, "I believe these people came expecting to see Tom Thumb and his wife."

Any suggestion of Robert's going into the army was sternly and tearfully opposed by his mother. "We have lost one son, and his loss is as much as I can bear, without being called upon to make another sacrifice," she would tearfully plead to the embarrassed President. Anxious himself to quit his studies and go to war, Robert visited his parents every few months.

On September 22, 1862, shortly after the Battle of Antietam, the President issued a preliminary statement that on January 1, 1863, he would free the slaves by proclamation. The First Lady rejoiced at the news.

In September Mrs. Lincoln visited New York City to do more shopping, staying at the Metropolitan Hotel; in November she visited New England. That month the Illinois Congressional elections indicated that the people in their home state were not behind the Administration. With Springfield still regarded as home, the Lincolns were disturbed and disappointed.

On December 21, while staying at the Continental Hotel in Philadelphia, the First Lady received a solicitous message from the President, "Do not come on the night train. It is too cold. Come in the morning."

It was a gloomy Christmas in the White House. Even the talkative Tad seemed strangely silent. Washington was filled with wounded and dying men. The Confederates had been successful in the fighting at Fredericksburg.

CHAPTER FIFTEEN

A DRAGON FOR A CHAMPION

On the first day of the New Year, 1863, the President issued his long-awaited Emancipation Proclamation. After greeting foreign diplomats and officialdom, the White House opened its doors to the man in the street.

On this most splendid of all Washington New Years, the President shook so many eager hands that he was forced to rest his fingers before they could grasp the Proclamation pen. Francis B. Carpenter painted the historic scene. The President's wife let her thoughts wander back to her Kentucky childhood and the slaves with their clanking chains en route for the Louisiana swamps.

News reporters had a field day; suddenly the Negro was a fashionable subject. Mary Clemmer Ames, prolific and barbed-tongued as ever, wrote a series of somewhat distorted articles entitled, "Emancipation in the District—Stories of the Late Slaves." In these she included Mrs. Keckley, although in fact the successful *modiste* had not been emancipated by Lincoln; she had bought her freedom years before. Lavish with adjectives, the female journalist called Mrs. Keckley

> a stately, stylish woman, cheek tawny, features regular . . .
> a face strong with intellect and heart . . . It is Lizzie who
> fashions those splendid costumes of Mrs. Lincoln, whose
> artistic elegance has been so highly praised during the
> last winter. Stately carriages stand before her door, whose

haughty owners sit before Lizzie docile as lambs, whilst she
tells them what to wear. Lizzie is an artist, and has such
a genius for making women look pretty that no one thinks
of disputing her decrees.

If Mary Clemmer Ames admired Mrs. Keckley, she showed no love for Mrs. Lincoln, of whom she declared,

While her sister-women scraped lint, sewed bandages and
put on nurses' caps, and gave their call to country and to
death, the wife of the President spent her time in rolling to
and from Washington and New York, intent on extravagant
purchases for herself and the White House.

In defending the First Lady from so vitriolic an attack, William Stoddard noted the long hours she had spent visiting the soldiers in the hospitals. However, he did think that she should have cultivated the friendship of the press.

If she were worldly wise, she would carry newspaper
reporters from two to five, of both sexes, every time she
went and she would have them take shorthand notes of
what she says to the sick soldiers and what the sick soldiers
say to her.

In spite of Mary Clemmer, the First Lady found a champion in another woman writer, once dubbed "Dragon of the Hesperides" by *The New York Times*. She was Jane Grey Swisshelm, of whom a contemporary editor warned: "Beware of Sister Jane."

Mrs. Swisshelm had been divorced for desertion by her patient, long-suffering husband. Her life is described by the nineteenth-century biographer, Phebe A. Hannaford, as being one of "shadow and struggle and triumph." Mrs. Swisshelm once declared, "Oh! But it is good to have lived and suffered and worked . . . nothing can go wrong with us if only we are right." She thought she was right in extolling the virtues of the most maligned First Lady, whose ardent champion she became. At first she had refused even to attend a Lincoln reception because "He had proved an obstructionist as well as an abolitionist and I felt no respect for him; while his wife was everywhere spoken of as a Southern woman with Southern sympathies—a conspirator against the Union." Now she wrote,

> I watched the President and Mrs. Lincoln receive. His sad, earnest, honest face was irresistable in its plea for confidence, and Mrs. Lincoln's manner was so simple and motherly, so unlike that of all Southern women I had seen, that I doubted the tales I had heard. Her head was not that of a conspirator. She would be incapable of successful deceit, and whatever her purposes were, they must be known to all who knew her. . . . I recognized Mrs. Lincoln as a loyal, liberty-loving woman, more staunch even than her husband in opposition to the Rebellion and its cause, and as my very dear friend for life.

The President's face looked sad yet there were still rare moments when he smiled and joked as in happier days. When the Prince of Wales was betrothed to the beautiful Princess Alexandra of Denmark, Queen Victoria sent President Lincoln a letter announcing the fact. This was duly presented to him by Lord Lyons, the British Ambassador.

After Lord Lyons had pompously made the announcement himself before even presenting his royal mistress's letter, the President ordered the astonished diplomat, "Lord Lyons, go thou and do likewise." He never forgot the look on the Ambassador's face, and that evening when they were alone, he shared the story with Mrs. Lincoln.

In great numbers the freed slaves flocked to Washington, which in many cases did not live up to their expectations. As Mrs. Keckley explained, "To them it was a beautiful vision, a land of sunshine, rest, and glorious promise." In the interests of the Relief Society she visited their camps, later reporting her experiences to Mrs. Lincoln. One old woman, fresh from plantation servitude, had come North quite believing President and Mrs. Lincoln to be the government. She loudly complained that she had been there eight months without Mrs. Lincoln giving her a shift, whereas her old mistress had provided her with two every year!

The First Lady was quick to rectify the omission. She helped Mrs. Keckley raise funds in aid of the Contraband Relief Association which had been originated to help clothe and feed those Negroes who were being turned free without one cent of their own. She was the first to give $200 to this cause, contributing also on many later occasions.

In a raging April snowstorm the President, his wife, and their younger son visited the army of the Potomac, where they received a stirring reception. Visibility being poor, they anchored for the night in a little cove opposite Indian Head. There were no guards aboard the boat and no precautions against being taken by surprise. Had the Confederates known, they could easily have captured the Chief Executive.

Later they proceeded to the headquarters of General Joseph Hooker, "the blond War God," where they were housed in three large hospital tents newly floored and furnished with camp beds for the occasion. Tad enjoyed himself, for the Cavalry allowed him to ride a horse. The President was glad of this brief respite from Washington, yet he confessed that "nothing touches the tired spot."

During the Lincolns' stay in camp the photograph of a Confederate officer with the inscription "A rebellious Rebel" on the back was brought into camp, addressed to General Averill, a former classmate of the sender. The Lincolns were much amused at the incident, and Mrs. Lincoln insisted that the rebel officer must be in rebellion against the rebel government. "No," said the President, "it means that the rebel officer wants everybody to know he is a double-dyed-in-the-wool sort of rebel, a rebel of rebels."

The 1863 campaign turned the tide of war in favor of the Federals, although May 2–4 at the great battle of Chancellorsville they were defeated. It was during this conflict that the Confederates lost a great general in Stonewall Jackson. On July 1 the conflicting armies met at Gettysburg where, after three days of desperate fighting, the Federals were again victorious. Meanwhile General Grant undertook the capture of Vicksburg which the Confederates had fortified. Its 30,000 men surrendered on July 4. In this battle, Mrs. Lincoln's half-brother David Todd—hated for his treatment of Union prisoners—was mortally wounded. Katharine Helm related how "his sister at the White House, with a frozen smile on her lips and a heart of lead, must listen to the shouts of rejoicing over Grant's victory."

While the Battle of Gettysburg was actually raging, the President's wife was involved in a serious accident. She was driving in her carriage when the coachman's seat broke, throwing him to the ground. The horses bolted; Mrs. Lincoln jumped out, striking the back of her head upon a sharp rock. Later it was found that the carriage seat screws had been deliberately removed to loosen the seat. She lay in bed with a badly cut head for three weeks. Robert believed that she never quite recovered from this fall. The President watched over his sick wife with much tenderness, overwhelming the trained nurse with gratitude for saving "Mother's" life.

The First Lady was still sick when news reached the White House that her youngest half-brother, red-headed Alex Todd whom she had enjoyed so much when he was a baby, had been killed in a skirmish at Baton Rouge. Once more she had to stifle her grief, but memories of the child Alex giving her the pick of his puppies kept coming back. His mother's illness was a great strain upon Tad, who missed his dead brother very much.

Mrs. Lincoln made a brief September visit to New York, when she stayed at the Fifth Avenue Hotel, then located at 23rd Street and Fifth Avenue, overlooking Madison Square Park. Fall had come early that year; already the maples were turning to gold. She was grateful for the President's insistence that she should take a change. Such pleasant relief was short-lived, for on September 20, General Ben Hardin Helm, husband of her much-loved half-sister Emilie, was killed at the Battle of Chickamauga. An honorable man, he visited the White House in 1861, only to refuse the Federal paymaster's commission offered him by the President. The President took Ben Helm's death hard, telling Senator David Davis, "I feel as David of old did when he was told of the death of Absalom."

It was three weeks before Governor Helm of Kentucky heard

of his son's death. He then contacted Emilie's mother, Betsy Todd, to write Mary in order to secure a pass for his daughter-in-law's return home. "I am totally at a loss to know how to begin," he told her.

The young widow, traveling with her little daughter Katherine, from the funeral in Atlanta, was stopped at Fort Monroe where she was told that unless she swore an oath of allegiance to the United States she could not proceed. Emilie refused, declaring that to do so would be treason to her dead husband's memory. Realizing that she was the President's sister-in-law, the officer concerned wired the White House for instructions as to what he should do. The President promptly telegraphed the reply, "Send her to me."

Dressed in deep mourning and heavily veiled, Emilie Helm arrived at the Executive Mansion where the two half-sisters embraced each other "in silence and tears." They dined alone when, says Emilie,

> Our tears gathered silently and fell unheeded as with choking voices we tried to talk of immaterial things. We talked of old friends in Springfield and in Kentucky. Allusion to the present is like tearing open a fresh and bleeding wound and the pain is too great for self-control. And the future, alas, the future seems empty, of everything but despair. So to gain anything like calmness we approach any subject timidly and wonder if anything we are about to say can give the other pain.

Afterwards the First Lady took her half-sister to see the East, Green, and Blue rooms. Emilie was particularly delighted to see the famed portrait of Washington that Dolley Madison had saved from the British, afterwards noting in her diary that "Dolly [sic] Madison's first husband was a Todd."

CHAPTER SIXTEEN

EMILIE'S VISIT

Emilie slept in the State Guest Chamber, which oppressed her with its purple hangings that seemed "gloomy and funereal though brightened with yellow cords." She felt the cold, but the Presidential fires were "cheerful and comfortable." Appreciative of all her half-sister's efforts to make her stay happy under the circumstances, she says,

> Sister is doing everything to distract my mind and her own from our terrible grief, but at times it overwhelms us; we can't get away from it, try as we will to be cheerful and accept fate. Sister has always a cheerful word and a smile for Mr. Lincoln, who seems thin and care-worn and seeing her sorrowful would add to his care.

Driving in the state carriage, somewhat nerve-racking to the First Lady after her recent accident, they suddenly came upon a streetcar from which some small boys were jumping. The White House coachman, unable to stop his horses in time, ran over one child, breaking his leg. When the carriage stopped, Mary jumped out crying, "Oh, the poor baby! Who is he, where does he live?" She tried to lift him into her arms, but a doctor who happened to be in the crowd said gently, "No, Mrs. Lincoln, you had better let me handle him. I will take him home." Not to be outdone, the First Lady followed the injured child, and consoled his mother, promising to return with some toys. Said Emilie, "Mary mothers all children." True to her promise, next day she returned laden with toys, fruit and a box of candy for the child.

During her stay Emilie bitterly complained.

> Sister and I cannot open our hearts to each other as freely as we would like. This frightful war comes between us like a barrier of granite closing our lips but not our hearts, for though our tongues are tied, we weep over our dead together and express through our clasped hands the sympathy we feel for each other in our mutual grief.
>
> Sister Mary and I avoid any reference to the war or to any of my experiences in the South for fear of hurting each other. Her fine tact and delicacy fill me with admiration. She can so quickly turn a dangerous subject into other channels.

They talked of Betsy, now very old, and Emilie states that Mary sent her many messages of love and sympathy. Mary was thinking of the loss of Alex, saying, "My heart bleeds for her, Emilie. . . . A wound in a mother's heart can never heal. I pray you will never have that sorrow to bear."

"Sister Mary's heart is particularly sore over the death of Alex," noted Emilie. "He was so young, so loving, so impetuous, our dear, red-headed, baby brother!"

Many times Emilie writes of the First Lady's kindness.

> Sister Mary's tenderness for me is very touching. She and Brother Lincoln pet me as if I were a child, and, without words, try to comfort me.

There were other times when, in her turn, the First Lady was in need of the comfort, such as the morning Emilie found her sitting "in a drooping despondent attitude." She had dropped her newspaper to the floor. Holding out her arms, the First Lady begged, "Kiss me, Emilie, and tell me that you love me! I seem to be the scape-goat for both North and South!" Then just as suddenly her mood changed; she held her head proudly and smiled.

Emilie was still marveling at the transformation when she heard Lincoln ask, "I hope you two are not planning some mischief!" Later he said, "Little sister, I hope you can come up and spend the summer with us at the Soldiers' Home. You and Mary love each other—it is good for her to have you with her." There was anxiety in his face as he continued, "I feel worried about Mary, her nerves have gone to pieces; she cannot hide from me that the strain she has been under has been too much for her mental as well as her physical health." Then he asked, "What do you think?"

Emilie replied, "She seems very nervous and excitable and once or twice when I have come into the room suddenly the frightened look in her eyes has appalled me. She seems to fear that other sorrows may be added to those we already have to bear. I believe if anything should happen to you or Robert or Tad it would kill her."

Lincoln asked her to stay with Mary for as long as she could, and confided that Mary suffered from "hallucinations." Emilie was soon to experience just what he was talking about. She writes,

> After I had said good-night and gone to my room last night, there was a gentle knock at the door and Sister Mary's voice said, "Emilie, may I come in?"
> [Mary then attempted to console Emilie on the recent death of her husband by telling her the dead still lived and could visit their loved ones.]
> "When my noble little Willie was first taken from me there was not a ray of light. . . . If Willie did not come to comfort me I would still be drowned in tears, and while I long inexpressibly to touch him, to hold him in my arms, and still grieve that he has no future in this world that I might watch with a mother's heart—he lives, Emilie. He comes to me every night and stands at the foot of my bed with the same sweet, adorable smile he has always had; he does not always come alone; little Eddie is sometimes with him, and twice he has come with our brother, Alex."

Emilie felt that it was unnatural and abnormal for Mary to behave in this manner. She was frightened for her sister, who seemed unusually wrought up.

When sorrows came to the Lincolns it seemed they came "not as single spies but in battalions." The President was so worried over his wife's health that when a friend told him that a scoundrel was deceiving the First Lady into using her influence for him, the President gravely replied, "The caprices of Mrs. Lincoln, I am satisfied, are the result of partial insanity." Then after a moment of silence he asked, "Is the malady beyond medical remedy to check before it becomes fully developed?" The visitor replied that he believed Mrs. Lincoln could still be helped by kindness and firmness.

Mary was just as worried about the President's state of health as he was about hers. "Emilie, what do you think of Mr. Lincoln," she asked. "Do you think he is well? I really think he looks very ill." Emilie tactfully answered that he seemed thinner than she had ever seen him. "Oh, Emilie," cried Mary, "will we ever awake from this hideous nightmare?" She looked long at her half-sister for a reply, but there was none forthcoming. "I did not answer," wrote Emilie, "for it does not seem possible we ever can."

Although Abraham and Mary did their best not to discuss the war in front of their tragic visitor, others were not so kind, particularly General Daniel E. Sickles and Senator Ira Harris of New York, who called one day at the Executive Mansion.

"Well, we have whipped the rebels at Chattanooga," said Harris gleefully, "and I hear, madam, that the scoundrels ran like scared rabbits."

The color drained from Emilie's face as she replied with as much dignity as she could muster, "It was the example, Senator Harris, that you set them at Bull Run and Manassas." Her throat was choking. Then the Senator turned upon the First Lady, demanding, "Why isn't Robert in the Army? He is old enough and strong enough to serve his country. He should have gone to the front some time ago."

Striving for self-control, the First Lady bit her lip. "Robert is making his preparations now to enter the Army, Senator Harris. He is not a shirker as you seem to imply for he has been anxious to go for a long time. If fault there be, it is mine. I have insisted that he should stay in college a little longer as I think an educated man can serve his country with more intelligent purpose than an ignoramus."

Emilie's Visit : : page 147

This reply did not please the Senator, who coldly told her, "I have only one son and he is fighting for his country." Then turning to Emilie with a bow he declared, "And, madam, if I had twenty sons they should all be fighting the rebels." This aroused Emilie's temper. "And if I had twenty sons, Senator Harris," she snapped, "they should all be opposing yours." Cold and trembling, she stumbled from the room, followed by the First Lady.

The President, however, had the last word. "The child has a tongue like the rest of the Todds," he mocked the infuriated Sickles.

"You should not have that rebel in your house," shouted General Sickles, slapping the table with his hand.

"Excuse me, General Sickles," replied the President with quiet dignity. "My wife and I are in the habit of choosing our own guests. We do not need from friends either advice or assistance in the matter. Besides the little rebel came because I ordered her to come; it was not of her own volition."

However, the incident showed Emilie that, kind though the Lincolns were, her presence in the White House was an embarrassment. Even the children, Tad and Katherine, were acting at times like "glaring little belligerents."

"This is the President," announced Tad proudly, showing his father's picture to his cousin.

"No," insisted Katherine, "that is not the President. Mr. Davis is President."

"Hurrah for Abe Lincoln," shouted Tad.

"Hurrah for Jeff Davis," came the defiant reply.

At last the President intervened. "Well, Tad," he said, "you know who is your President, and I am your little cousin's Uncle Lincoln."

The children were still glaring at one another as he placed them one upon each knee.

Emilie's White House stay lasted barely a week. Giving her a paper of safe conduct, the President said, "Little Sister, I never knew you to do a mean thing in your life. I know you will not embarrass me in any way on your return to Kentucky."

"Nothing," says Emilie, "was said to me then or afterwards about taking the oath of allegiance."

CHAPTER SEVENTEEN

A SECOND TERM

The fall weather that year seemed to invigorate Mary so the President was delighted when she agreed to accompany him to Grover's Theater on October 17. To aid the United States Sanitary Commission, the greatest American actress of her generation, Charlotte Saunders Cushman, was appearing in her famous role, Lady Macbeth. This worthy organization raised funds to provide comforts for the Union troops and the performance climaxed Washington's grand Sanitary Fair.

In her youth, Charlotte Cushman was a poor Boston girl whose mother, Mary Eliza Babbit Cushman, had by sheer will power pushed her talented daughter to stardom. The President had met the mannish-looking actress in 1861 when, as a close friend of the Seward family, she had called upon him at the White House. At that time she became so excited that she forgot the favor she had come to ask him. She was actually seeking a West Point placement for the son of a friend. After taking leave of "true and faithful" Lincoln, as she called the President, Miss Cushman informed Seward, "When you did me the honor to present me, I was so completely taken up with him and his humor that I forgot my mission and came away."

James William Wallack, Jr., played Macbeth and Edward Loomis Davenport, Macduff. Charlotte Cushman's personal copy of the program, fringed in lace, bordered in blue, and printed in red upon white satin, survives among her papers in the Library of Congress.

A Second Term :: page 149

The President, who was delighted with the performance, had written a few months previously, "I think nothing equals Macbeth."

The Washington *Evening Star* on Monday, October 19, 1863, faithfully described the great event.

> The benefit in aid of the Sanitary Commission, at Grover's Saturday night was a great success, netting over $2,000 for the object proposed. President Lincoln, Master Thady [Thomas] Lincoln, and Mr [William O.] Stoddard, the President's Private Secretary, occupied the lower stage boxes to the right, and Secretary Seward, Lord Lyons (British Minister) and others of note, those opposite. Every part of the house was jammed, and reserved seats sold at a large premium long before the hour of opening.

Manager Grover gave $2,018, the entire receipts of the evening, to the Sanitary Commission.

Lincoln was concerned over the chances of his re-election, for although he had legislated for an end to slavery, he had as yet found no solution to ending the war. Already the North, weary of three years' fighting, was beset with disloyalty and dissension. The President was being blamed for the war.

The Presidential ambitions of Salmon P. Chase, Secretary of the Treasury, were no idle threat. To combat his maneuvers, the Union League Club arranged an early convention for June 7, 1864, before the Chase supporters were able to gather full strength. Mainly as a result, Lincoln's second nomination was successfully secured. When the President refused to pick a running mate, thus emphasizing the objective of unity, members of the convention chose Democrat Andrew Johnson from the secession state of Tennessee.

After Chase's attempt to usurp his chief's position, to have him remain in the Cabinet was an intolerable situation. To the First Lady's delight he resigned. Her pleasure was short-lived, however, for the President seldom harbored malice for long. Later in the year he appointed Chase as Chief Justice.

The following month, the Confederates under General Jubal Early made an unsuccessful surprise expedition against Washington. Secretary of War Stanton ordered the President and his family back to the White House from their vacation at the Soldiers' Home. The First Lady accompanied her husband to Fort Stevens where, with other spectators, they actually witnessed the troops in action. With his usual disregard for personal safety, the President exposed the upper part of his long body above the parapet where, less than three feet away, a surgeon was killed by a sharpshooter's bullet. The President still remaining exposed when everyone else had taken cover, General Horatio Wright politely ordered him to withdraw. Not so Lieutenant-Colonel Oliver Wendell Holmes, who shouted, "Get down, you fool!" On September 3 there was a turning point in the war: Atlanta, under Sherman's ruthless hammering, fell at last.

Early that same September Mary heard with some interest of the dramatic death of Rose O'Neal Greenhow. Mrs. Greenhow, upon her release from imprisonment in Washington, had been escorted to the South. There she immediately resumed her colorful activities, first visiting General Beauregard in Charleston before sailing for France upon a blockade runner. In Paris she was honored by a private audience with the Emperor Napoleon III, and even managed to be presented to Queen Victoria, who had read the Greenhow opus, *My Imprisonment*. Mrs. Greenhow was said to have engaged herself to a British peer when she made an unfortunate decision to revisit the Confederacy, sailing in August, 1864, upon the *Condor*.

Running the blockade off Wilmington, North Carolina, the steamer hit a bar and stuck fast. Fearing the arrival of Federal ships, Mrs. Greenhow, together with two Confederate agents, requested they be set ashore. Their boat had hardly been lowered into the water when it was overturned by a wave. Mrs. Greenhow had secured a bag of gold sovereigns around her waist, the weight of which proved her undoing, and she was drowned. Her body was washed up next day, and she was buried with the full honors of war in Wilmington. Her daughter became an actress, married, and settled in California.

A Second Term :: page 151

Election Day, 1864, was a very wet one. The President and his wife awaited news of the results in a White House that seemed strangely deserted. Unable to work because of the suspense, the President was persuaded by Tad to watch the guard of loyal Bucktails lining up in the rain to vote for him. Washington itself was unusually quiet. Men with their trousers rolled up out of the wet went into the streets hoping for news.

At seven in the evening the President set out for the War Department, where, late at night, he heard that his re-election seemed assured. A little supper followed at which he "went awkwardly and hospitably to work shoveling out the fried oysters."

Toward the end of 1864 the President—himself a person of humble background—was intrigued by the tale of the young post office clerk, Vinnie Ream, now a protégée of the eminent sculptor, Clark Mills. Her long-time ambition was to sculpt a head of the President, a request which was granted, providing she would not expect him to pose. Instead she was to observe him as he worked at his desk.

Vinnie sent her tools and a large tub of clay to the White House. The result was destined to be one of the finest Lincoln likenesses ever made. While working, she noticed how he often crossed to the window, looking out to where his dead child used to play. Even then, long after the boy had gone, the President still seemed to be "watching for Willie. . . . Sometimes," Vinnie goes on to say, "great tears rolled down his cheeks." Although the First Lady had once told General Adam Badeau, "Do you know, sir, that I never permit the President to see any woman alone?" she seems to have had no objection to his "sitting" for the seventeen-year-old girl.

Tad, then a boy of nearly twelve, often visited his father's study while Vinnie was working, to make a critical examination of her progress. She noted his long, grown-up gold watch-chain and neatly parted hair.

On March 4, 1865, Lincoln's second Inaugural Address included the lines destined to live long after him: "With malice toward none, with charity for all, with firmness in the right as God gives us to see the right, let us strive to finish the work we are in."

The actual Inauguration was somewhat spoiled by the Vice President, Andrew Johnson, who, weak from a recent attack of typhoid fever, became intoxicated from a drink he had taken before the ceremony. At the Inaugural White House levee, so many people crowded into the mansion to shake Lincoln's hand that his glove was quickly soiled. The First Lady gave it to Mrs. Keckley as a memento.

Among the many wishing to greet the President were numerous Negroes, yet surprisingly, unknown to either of the Lincolns, orders had been given not to admit them. A member of Congress, seeing the eloquent Negro orator, Frederick Douglass, on the outskirts of the crowd, inquired if he had yet greeted the President. When told the reason why he had not, the irate Congressman worked his way through the crowds to the President, who immediately had Douglass admitted to his presence. Pressing his hand warmly, President Lincoln said, "Mr. Douglass, I am glad to meet you. I have long admired your course, and I value your opinions highly."

When the last guests had departed, the Lincolns were horrified at the damage they had left behind. The First Lady was in tears, for it seemed that all her refurbishing of the White House had been in vain. A square yard of expensive red brocade from the East Room draperies had been cut out; the same thing had happened in the Green Room. As for the lace curtains, enterprising guests had diligently snipped out the embossed flowers. William Crook, a White House bodyguard, remarked that it "looked as if a regiment of rebel troops had been quartered there—with permission to forage."

On the following Monday, while dressing her for a belated Inaugural Ball, Mrs. Keckley told the First Lady how pleased Frederick Douglass had been with his presentation. At once she turned, pouting, to her husband.

"Father," she asked, "why was not Mr. Douglass introduced to me?"

"I do not know. I thought he was presented."

"But he was not."

A Second Term : : page 153

"It must have been an oversight then, Mother," apologized the President. "I am sorry you did not meet him."

Mrs. Lincoln wore a shimmering dress of white silk and lace that had cost two thousand dollars, together with an elaborate fan of ermine and silver spangles, and a headdress made of white jessamine and purple violets. Although it was the First Lady's undisputed night of triumph over the ambitious Kate Chase, she was not altogether happy.

"Now that we have won the position," she murmured, "I almost wish it were otherwise. Poor Mr. Lincoln is looking so brokenhearted, so completely worn out, I fear he will not get through the next four years."

To Harriet Beecher Stowe, whose *Uncle Tom's Cabin* had played no small part in sparking the War between the States, the President confided, "I shall never live to see peace; this war is killing me." The fear of death was also preying upon the First Lady's mind, for during that March of 1865 she spent one thousand dollars on mourning clothes, along with her other Inaugural extravagances!

There was a happier circumstance that evening, in the presence of Robert Todd's partner for the evening, pretty Mary Harlan, daughter of the Iowa senator. Robert, inducted at last into the army, was now serving upon Grant's staff.

Supper was served shortly after midnight—if it could be described as having been served, for although Balzer, the confectioner, had provided for three hundred guests to eat at a sitting, the crowd of four thousand descended at once upon the tables. In no time the culinary displays were in a shambles. Gentlemen fought like little boys for their turkey neck trophies, while ladies ruined their costly gowns with grease and sticky pastries. Broken glasses and dishes littered the floor. A sugared ship of state was reduced to fragments, a feminine guest making off with an entire sugar horse. The only consolation for Mr. Balzer and Mrs. Lincoln was the safety of his *pièce de résistance*, a model of the Capitol which was removed before the food battle began!

CHAPTER EIGHTEEN

A PRESIDENT PASSES

The President was tired; at times he looked old and feeble, and his state of health had been noticed by the press. Deploring the host of new office-seekers, the *National Republican* suggested running them from the city before the President had a breakdown. With the war going in the Union's favor, the President was now besieged with turncoats and pardon-seekers. When on Thursday, March 23, at the invitation of General Grant, the Lincolns suddenly departed for the front, Washington buzzed with rumors that peace was being negotiated.

Hostilities had climaxed at Petersburg and Richmond. Sheridan's army had swung south to join Grant. Grant, Sherman, and Sheridan all conferred with the President aboard the *River Queen*.

Embarking on the *River Queen* for City Point, Virginia, Mrs. Lincoln could not have expected to be gone long for she invited Senator Charles Sumner to accompany them on March 29 to an evening performance of the Italian opera *Ernani*.

In addition to close friends such as Mrs. Keckley, the Lincolns had taken a large official party aboard with them. The dressmaker was delighted at the thought of visiting old friends newly emancipated, for City Point was near her birthplace, Petersburg. While the *River Queen* lay off City Point, Petersburg was evacuated.

While at City Point the Lincolns were driving together along the banks of the James River when they came to a tree-studded country graveyard. The enclosure was filled with masses of pink and white blossoms, while in the near distance sounded the peaceful lap of water. Stopping the carriage, the Lincolns walked hand in hand among the peaceful graves. Suddenly the President, overcome with emotion, said, "Mary, you are younger than I. You will survive me. When I am gone, lay my remains in some quiet place like this."

Leaving Tad with his father, Mrs. Lincoln impulsively decided to return to Washington for a weekend. In doing so she missed her husband's dramatic entry into a still blazing Richmond on April 4. The *Atlantic Monthly*'s correspondent, C. C. Coppin, recorded the scene, telling of some forty or fifty freed black men working on the banks of a canal. Deserting their officer, they rushed to surround the President.

Says Coppin, "What cared those freed-men, fresh from the house of bondage, for floating timber and military commands? Their deliverer had come—he who next to the Lord Jesus was their best friend. It was not a hurrah that they gave, but a wild, jubilant cry of inexpressible joy."

Later, when Mary rejoined them, Tad had plenty to tell his mother of this and other stirring events. She saw much devastation done to the beautiful Virginia countryside while driving with her husband and Senator and Mrs. Harlan, with whom they had become close friends.

The First Lady's stay at City Point was marred by her bouts of jealousy. Previously, she had always managed to control such emotional outbursts; at least they were not manifested in public. Now suddenly it seemed that she could no longer contain them. The sight of the President even greeting another woman became anathema to her.

When she heard that the wife of a young officer had been given special permission by Lincoln to stay at the front she flew into a terrible rage, inferring that this kindly routine act was instead a mark of her husband's favor. But this outburst was nothing compared to the one that took place when she was to have participated with the President in a field inspection of Grant's troops.

The First Lady arrived in a carriage accompanied by General Grant and his devoted wife Julia Dent Grant, only to see the President on horseback, riding beside the beautiful wife of the post commander, General Edward Ord. Believing the troops would mistake Mrs. Ord for herself, the First Lady screamed at Mrs. Grant, "What does this woman mean by riding by the side of the President? Does she suppose that he wants her by the side of him?"

Kindly Mrs. Grant tried in vain to soothe the distraught woman, who retorted, "I suppose you think you'll get to the White House yourself, don't you?" Mrs. Grant was stunned into silence. Unsuspectingly, Mrs. Ord rode up, to be met with such a torrent of spleen and abuse that she retreated in tears.

Next day the First Lady did not appear in public, the President personally making her excuses and explaining that she was not well. Always before, outside of her home, the First Lady had managed to control her temper.

During the weekend of April 9, when Lee was surrendering to Grant at Appomattox, the Lincolns returned to the White House. The President was still weary. Sleeping badly, he was again troubled with nightmares, seeing in one of them a soldier guarding a casket in the East Room. "The President was killed by an assassin," he explained. Abraham told Mary nothing of this but it worried him.

On the day following their return the President was scarcely through breakfast when noisy, good-natured crowds surrounded the White House, shouting for his appearance. Absorbed by his dreams of rebuilding the battered Union, he ordered the musicians to play the South's own *Dixie*.

On the Tuesday evening all important government buildings were illuminated, just as they had been to commemorate the fall of Richmond. Even the ominous First Street prison and the Insane Asylum glittered like giant stars. Gas jets and candles combined to give the whole Capital a gala mood. Across the Potomac, General Lee's mansion was ablaze with lights, while happy throngs of freed Negroes surged over the lawns singing *The Year of Jubilee*.

From a White House window the President addressed the crowds, a noble speech containing his tolerant views on Reconstruction. The crowd, drunk with victory, were in no mood for such reasoning. Even the Radicals in his own Republican party thought their President's views on Negro suffrage far too liberal. Lincoln was glad when he could step indoors again and close the casement, for he wanted to be with his wife and Tad. Among the hundreds of spectators was a tall, thin man whose heart was sickened by the

President's words of tolerance. His name was John Wilkes Booth, an actor, brother of the more famous actor Edwin Booth.

On Friday evening—Good Friday—the First Lady had planned a theater party at Ford's where Miss Laura Keene was appearing in Tom Taylor's dated comedy *Our American Cousin*. As Florence Trenchard, Miss Keene had made this portrayal the most outstanding in her distinguished career.

The Grants had been invited to join the Presidential party but had declined, for Mrs. Grant was still smarting from the First Lady's acid tongue. At short notice in their place Mary invited a young engaged couple, Major Henry Rathbone and Miss Clara Harris, the stepson and daughter of Senator Ira Harris of New York. It was arranged that an armed guard should stay in the passageway leading to the Presidential box.

War Secretary Stanton and his wife, also invited to attend, sent their regrets. Mrs. Stanton was no friend of the First Lady; she did not even call upon her. Stanton himself loathed the theater, and was always begging the President not to expose himself so openly to danger.

Early that afternoon Vinnie Ream worked as usual for half an hour at the White House. Her clay model of the President's head was nearly finished. Lincoln graciously told "the mere slip of a girl" how delighted he was by her efforts. She had captured a sense of grief, compassion, and sympathy in her all-but-completed work.

Then although the weather had turned raw, cold, and gusty, the President took his accustomed drive with Mrs. Lincoln. When she asked if he wished to invite somebody to accompany them he replied, "No, I prefer to ride by ourselves today."

It was one of the happiest drives they had ever taken together. "We must be cheerful in the future, Mary," he gently told her. "Between the war and the loss of our darling Willie we have been very miserable."

"I have not seen you so happy since before Willie's death," she told him.

"Mary," he replied, "we have had a hard time of it since we came to Washington, but the war is over, and with God's blessing we may hope for four years of peace and happiness, and then we will go back to Illinois and pass the rest of our lives in quiet. We

The Lincoln bedroom at the White House as it is today. *White House Collection.*

have laid by some money, and during this term we will try and save up more, but I shall not have enough to support us. We will go back to Illinois and I will open a law office at Springfield or Chicago and practice law and at least do enough to help give us a livelihood."

Then they discussed a possible trip to Europe and the Holy Land. "I especially want to see Jerusalem," the President said.

It was late afternoon when they arrived back at the White House. Crossing the lawn towards the Treasury was a group of old friends, including Richard Oglesby, then governor of Illinois.

"Come back, boys, come back!" the President called out to them. Mary smiled that Abraham should still call such dignified men "boys."

When she had retired to her room to rest she could still hear her husband laughing and joking with his friends. It was like old times and she was delighted. Later Governor Oglesby recalled the scene.

> Lincoln got to reading some humorous book—I think it was by "John Phoenix." They kept sending for him to come to dinner. He promised each time to go, but would continue reading the book. Finally he got a sort of peremptory order that he must come to dinner at once. It was explained to me by the old man at the door that they were going to have dinner and then go to the theater.

The Lincolns were late leaving the White House for Abraham seemed loath to bid his friends goodnight. The theater was nearly filled, but the stage boxes remained empty. House lights were already dimmed and the curtains raised by two young Negroes before the Presidential party arrived. It was 8:30 P.M. when they entered the theater.

The guard assigned to protect the President, John F. Parker, had a poor record with the Metropolitan Police. Some months earlier he had been charged with being drunk and disorderly in a house of ill-repute. His chair, placed in the passageway from the Dress Circle to the Presidential box, did not enjoy a view of the stage and Parker longed to see the play. He deserted his post to watch.

A Rose for Mrs. Lincoln : : page 160

The President was comfortably seated in a red upholstered rocking chair which young Harry Ford was especially fond of, having used it in his own bedroom. A sofa and some easy chairs brought from the property and reception rooms added a touch of elegance. American flags were tied at the sides and the middle column of the lace-curtained double box. Draped across the railing in front was another Stars and Stripes, in the middle of which Harry had placed a portrait of George Washington.

The Lincolns and their young guests were in a happy mood. The President and his wife chatted between acts. Impulsively Mary drew nearer to her husband, clasping his large hand in her own.

"What will Miss Harris think of my hanging on to you so?" she whispered.

"She won't think anything about it," Abraham reassured her.

The assassin Booth had little trouble in entering the Presidential box, for Parker had left it quite unguarded. The occupants were engrossed in the play, now well into Act Three, Scene Two. Asa Trenchard, a bumpkin, had just been informed by his aristocratic English cousin that he did not know the manners of good society.

"Don't know the manners of good society," Asa grumbled. "Well, I guess I know enough to turn you inside out, old gal—you sockdolagizing old mantrap."

These ridiculous lines were the last words that Abraham Lincoln ever heard, for at that moment Booth raised his tiny derringer and fired. One single shot sent a homemade lead pellet into the President's brain. Lincoln never even saw his attacker. Major Rathbone grabbed at the assassin, only to be slashed on the arm with a knife. Booth then leaped over the railing, dropping onto the stage twelve feet below.

"*Sic semper tyrannis*—thus it shall ever be for tyrants!" he shouted at the shocked audience. Then in an instant he was gone.

As the assassin fired, Mary felt Abraham's warm hand go limp in her own.

They carried the dying President across the street to the nearest bed in the house of a stranger. Laura Keene's dress was stained with blood where she had cradled the injured President. An irate mob was yelling, "Burn the theater."

All night long rain poured down on the anxious crowds outside. There had been three doctors in the theater. Others were summoned, including Mrs. Lincoln's cousin and good friend, Dr. Beecher Todd of Lexington.

The First Lady was half-crazed with hysteria and sorrow. Messengers were dispatched to find Mrs. Keckley, without success. She was in fact out hunting for Mrs. Lincoln, but the White House guard refused to divulge her whereabouts. Robert, who had arrived in Washington only that day, was also summoned.

Mrs. James Dixon, wife of Senator Dixon of Connecticut, was one of four women who shared the First Lady's terrible vigil. All through the night she continually fainted, reviving to cover her unconscious husband's face with kisses and screaming for him to speak one word, to let her die with him. It was no good. At 7:22 on the morning of April 15, Abraham Lincoln, Sixteenth President of the United States passed into history. As a doctor placed silver dollar pieces upon his eyes Mary Lincoln sobbed, "O my God, and have I given my husband to die?"

The bells were already tolling when they led her to her carriage, crying at the sight of Ford's, "Oh that dreadful house! that dreadful house!" Although under doctors' orders to be put to bed immediately, Mrs. Dixon notes, "She refused to go into any of the rooms she had previously occupied. 'Not there! Oh, not there!' she said—and so we took her to the one she had arranged for the President for a summer home to write in."

It was there that Mrs. Keckley found Abraham's widow tossing uneasily upon the bed. "The room was darkened," says Mrs. Keckley, "and Mrs. Lincoln was being attended by the wife of Secretary Welles who was only too thankful to be relieved of her unpleasant task."

As soon as she had managed to quiet her bereaved friend, Mrs. Keckley slipped out to see the late President's body. "The Moses of my people had fallen in the hour of his triumph" was her reaction as she lifted the white cloth that covered his face. She found it "beautiful as well as grandly solemn."

A Rose for Mrs. Lincoln : : page 162

On returning, Mrs. Keckley found Mrs. Lincoln hysterical again. Robert was trying to comfort his mother, while little Tad crouched at the foot of the bed. Mrs. Keckley recorded her own sense of horror.

> I shall never forget the scene—the wails of a broken heart, the unearthly shrieks, the terrible convulsions, the wild, tempestuous outbursts of grief from the soul. I bathed Mrs. Lincoln's head with cold water, and soothed the terrible tornado as best I could. Tad's grief at his father's death was as great as the grief of his mother, but her terrible outbursts awed the boy into silence. Sometimes he would throw his arms around her neck, and exclaim: "Don't cry so, Mamma! don't cry, or you will make me cry, too! You will break my heart."

Mrs. Lincoln discovered one evening that the guard assigned to protect her was that same Parker who had neglected his duty in order to see the play. She turned on him like a tigress. "So you are on guard tonight—on guard in the White House after helping to murder the President!"

People came and went but still she stayed in her darkened room. On Monday afternoon the embalmers had completed their work. Lincoln lay in his new black suit in the White House guest room. Now it was as if he no longer belonged to his family but to the nation. The total expenses for the funeral, paid by the government, came to thirty thousand dollars.

On Tuesday the body in its silver-starred casket was carried into the East Room and placed upon the black-festooned catafalque, just as Lincoln had dreamed. The great and the lowly paid silent tribute, yet still the widow remained a wraithlike figure in her room.

Captain Robert Lincoln and Tad attended the funeral service held in the East Room on Wednesday. Then the anchor of roses was removed and the casket taken to the Capitol. For another day the body lay in state under the high dome. Early on Friday morning, before the city was properly awake, it was removed to the railroad depot, where it was joined by Willie's small casket, taken from a cemetery vault. The long journey home to Springfield had begun.

For five long weeks Mary Todd Lincoln remained cloistered in her White House room, watched over by the faithful Mrs. Keckley. Once she sent a message to the people of Springfield forbidding them to bury her husband in a public place where she might not lie beside him.

Downstairs, a continual rabble of souvenir hunters roamed at large through the state rooms, carting off anything that took their fancy. Silver and dining ware disappeared, as well as choice ornaments and even heavy pieces of furniture. Expensive sofas, chairs, and draperies were cut to threads by human vultures. While all this was going on, Mrs. Lincoln refused to see anybody but the servants. Box after box of her personal effects daily left the White House, giving rise to rumors that she was illegally taking into retirement national treasures which in fact were being plundered as she mourned.

The United States had paid for her mourning apparel which amounted to $142.50. Tad's black felt hat cost $4.50 more. His mourning band was fifty cents!

All her efforts to improve the furnishings of the White House were lost in the final tragedy. Only the gigantic Lincoln bed and a few other things remained to delight the eyes of future generations.

Lincoln's last journey from the White House had drawn vast crowds to the Executive Mansion. Now it was the turn of the wife who, in spite of her jealous and erratic nature, he had loved so well. Walking slowly down the public stairway, she entered her carriage without once looking back. There were no bands, no crowds to wish her well. With her sons she drove to the railroad depot to board a train for Chicago. Said Mrs. Keckley, who accompanied them, "The silence was painful."

The Tomb of Abraham and Mary Todd Lincoln, Springfield, Illinois.

CHAPTER NINETEEN

THE EXILE

The Widow Lincoln was accompanied on her long journey to Chicago by her two sons, the faithful Mrs. Keckley, and Dr. Anson G. Henry, a lifetime friend, who upon hearing of the President's death had immediately hurried to the side of "poor heartbroken Mrs. Lincoln." To his own wife he said, "Poor Mrs. Lincoln was not only proud of her husband; she loved him with an intensity possible only to such a high-strung, passionate temperament."

Mrs. Lincoln's excessive mourning was the custom of the age. She had a counterpart in the Queen of England, Victoria, who had gone into rigid seclusion following the death of her own husband, the Prince Consort. It was hard on the relatives for, after a most exacting journey West, during which time Mrs. Lincoln was afflicted by terrible migraine headaches, they settled briefly at the Tremont House before moving to another less expensive lodging in Hyde Park. These quarters were so small and dismal that Robert complained bitterly that he "would almost as soon be dead as be compelled to remain three months in this dreary house." Even Mrs. Keckley found them trying, and soon returned to her home in Washington. It was then that the widow deliberately hid from relatives and old friends who might have helped her.

"I still remain closeted in my rooms, take an occasional walk in the park and as usual see no one. . . . I cannot express how lonely and desolate we are," she wrote Dr. Henry, who had also gone home, in July.

To another loyal friend, Mrs. Gideon Welles, she confided, Day by day, I miss my beloved husband, more and more. How, I am, to pass through life without *him* who loved us so dearly, it is impossible for me to say. . . . I must patiently await, the hour, when, "God's Love," shall place me, by *his* side again. Where there are no more partings and *no more* tears shed. For I have become almost blind, with weeping.

Queen Victoria and the Empress Eugénie of France both sent her understanding letters of sympathy. From England came a scrapbook containing resolutions and speeches concerning Lincoln, made after his death. It pleased her so much that she told Charles Sumner, another friend of long standing, "*Their* eyes were only beginning to comprehend the nature and nobility of the great, good man, who had accomplished his work, and before *his Judge*, it was pronounced complete."

Into the darkened rooms were brought the bills, already long overdue, from her creditors for all the clothing she had bought in her psychopathic fight to show the unfriendly Washington matrons that she was good as they. Now, no longer the wife of the President, there was nothing to stop them from harassing her. In desperation she enlisted the help of young Alexander Williamson, Willie and Tad's much-loved Scottish tutor in happier White House days. From June, 1865, until the close of 1867, she poured out her financial worries to him in writing. She did not want David Davis, Lincoln's able administrator to know of the money she owed, in case he might deplete the estate by paying it. Actually Lincoln, who died without making a will, had left an estate of more than eighty-three thousand dollars which, under the administrator's careful handling, had grown to over one hundred and ten thousand by the time he made a final accounting in 1868. Mary and her two sons would each receive a third of this. In spite of these figures, large for their day, the widow worried herself into a frenzy that she was impoverished. She could not think rationally any more where money was concerned.

She did not try to ignore her debts; she wanted to get them paid. Finally she came to the conclusion that a public subscription should be raised to help her. As she pointed out to Alexander Williamson,

> Notwithstanding my great and good husband's life, was sacrificed for his country, we are left to struggle, in a manner entirely new to us—and a noble people would pronounce our manner of life, *undeserved*. Roving Generals have elegant mansions showered upon them, and the American people—leave the family of the Martyred President, to struggle as best they may! Strange justice this.

Of course, being unaware of her large debts, the public, when they learned of Lincoln's large estate, could not understand such reasoning. Williamson had his hands full. Mary sent him letter after letter, even imploring him to plead with certain Washington stores to take back goods she had purchased.

A one-dollar subscription had been started in her behalf even before she left the White House. In time, ten thousand dollars from this source was given her. Toward the close of 1865, Congress voted her one year's Presidential salary which, after some deductions, came to just over twenty-two thousand dollars. She used it to buy a house, but on her limited income, she was unable to maintain it. She stated that her own income and that of her sons was from fifteen to eighteen hundred dollars each which, with the high interest rates, was correct. Mary had refused to return to the family home at Springfield because of all its memories of her husband.

In July of 1865 she suffered another heavy personal blow when her friend and mentor Dr. Henry was lost at sea en route for Olympia, Washington. She wrote Mrs. Henry that they had lost "two of the best men and the most devoted husbands."

She was now staying at the Clifton House in Chicago. A bad warehouse fire had occurred in December, one block from the warehouse where her effects were stored, including Lincoln memorabilia. Frantically she wrote Mrs. Welles, "The precious relics, belonging to my husband, are a continual source of anxiety to me." She wrote Mrs. Welles from her bed, having just returned from Springfield to see her husband's casket transferred from a public receiving vault into a new one. "When my good cousin—Mr. John Stuart, pointed to the vacant niche, by my beloved husband's side which he said, was reserved for me . . . I prayed, that my own appointed time, would not be far distant."

The trip to Springfield had made her ill. She had scarcely recovered when another demon arose to plague her in the form of that old adversary, William H. Herndon, the man who had once likened her to a snake. Overnight Herndon, Lincoln's Springfield law partner, had become a celebrity. Lincoln's death was the most important event in his life, for his reminiscences of the late President were being quoted all over the country. He had also designated himself as Lincoln's psychoanalyst.

He proposed writing a biography of Lincoln, which meant meeting the great man's widow. To this end he wrote Robert Lincoln asking for an appointment, which Mary, putting aside past differences, gladly agreed to. They were to meet at the St. Nicholas Hotel, in Springfield. She even wrote him, "In my overwhelming bereavement, those who loved my idolized husband . . . are very precious to me and mine."

When they eventually met in September, 1866, Lincoln's widow was horrified to find that Herndon had been drinking so heavily that his breath reeked of alcohol. He came with pen and paper ready to write down "as well as I could, the *substance* of what she said."

Knowing that Herndon had not been familiar with Lincoln the President but only with Lincoln the lawyer, she spoke of her husband's unselfish conduct during the nation's wartime travail. Proudly she told how "he rose grandly with the circumstances of the case, and men soon learned that he was above them all. . . . I never saw a man's mind develop himself so finely. . . . Mr. Lincoln had a kind of poetry in his nature."

The crafty Herndon was not interested in such lofty notions or in stories of Lincoln the President and family man. He was out for data of a more controversial and sensational nature. He promptly "examined," as he called it, Mrs. Lincoln on the subject of her husband's religion. Had he joined a church? Mary in all honesty said that he had not. Later Herndon credited her with saying that her husband was not a "technical Christian." Horrified, Mary knew this to be a term she had never used.

The Exile : : page 169

Apart from the interview with the widow, Herndon's romantic mind was trying to prove that before Lincoln had married Mary Todd he had left his heart in the grave of a young New Salem, Illinois, girl, Ann Rutledge. Herndon saw fit to forget the fact that at the time of her death Ann was still engaged to a certain John McNamar. McNamar himself had never heard of a romantic entanglement between Lincoln and Ann. Absent from New Salem at the time of her early death, he was returning with the express purpose of marrying her. In writing he states, "I never heard . . . [any] person say that Mr. Lincon (*sic*) addressed Miss Ann Rutledge in terms of courtship neither her own family nor my acquaintances otherwise." McNamar even carved her initials upon the headstone for her grave.

Herndon thought otherwise. He did not find it hard to make the country people of New Salem "recall" what had supposedly happened some thirty years before. "Men and women are inquisitive and hint a thing to them only and they will flesh the story falsely seen to suit the demands of the mind," he told Jesse Weik, his collaborator.

Lecturing in Springfield, November 16, 1866, he declared that "Abraham Lincoln loved Miss Ann Rutledge with all his soul, mind and strength . . ." while she "loved him as dearly." In Chicago, Lincoln's widow received the news that Herndon had publicly stated that her husband had never loved her. It was an awful blow to one already in such a confused state of mind. Writing David Davis to visit Herndon and "direct his *wandering* mind," she noted emphatically,

> As you justly remark, each and every one has had a little romance in their early days—but as my husband was *truth itself,* and as he always assured me, he had cared for no one but myself . . . I shall assuredly remain firm in my conviction that *Ann Rutledge* is a myth—for in all his confidential communications, such a romantic name, was never breathed. . . . Nor did his life or his joyous laugh, lead one to suppose his heart, was in any unfortunate woman's grave—but in the proper place with his loved wife and children.

A Rose for Mrs. Lincoln : : *page 170*

Unfortunately the damage was done; all the world loves a lover and the Lincoln–Rutledge saga was no exception. Ironically, today on the grave of the woman who, in all probability, had she lived a little longer, would have been Mrs. John McNamar, Edgar Lee Masters's poem reads:

> Out of me unworthy and unknown
> The vibrations of deathless music!
> "With malice toward none, with charity for all."
> Out of me forgiveness of millions toward millions,
> And the beneficent face of a nation
> Shining with justice and truth.
> I am Ann Rutledge, who sleep beneath these weeds,
> Beloved of Abraham Lincoln,
> Wedded to him, not through union
> But through separation
> Bloom forever, O Republic,
> From the dust of my bosom.

Even the State of the Union, it seemed, had to be grateful to the unfortunate Miss Rutledge.

No wonder some wag penned a fitting parody:

> Out of Herndon's spite and mental ramblings
> The vibrations of a deathless legend,
> With malice toward Mary, wife of Lincoln.
> Out of this legend millions upon millions
> Of readers, listeners, audiences at plays,
> Erase the love that Lincoln bore his wife,
> His many tender years of full devotion,
> And give that love to Ann, innocent usurper.
>
> This is Ann Rutledge who sleeps beneath these weeds,
> Beloved of and betrothed to John McNamar.
> Lincoln, the friend of both, grieved when she died;
> That tells the story; but the legend blooms forever
> Out of the quirks and hate in Herndon's bosom.

During this same year, 1866, the newspapers had diligently followed the controversial appointment of an American sculptor or

The Exile : : page 171

sculptress to make Lincoln's statue, to be placed in the Capitol's Rotunda.

Mary Lincoln's friend and champion, Jane Grey Swisshelm had espoused the cause of Harriet Hosmer, the Massachusetts sculptress, and was duly horrified when, on August 30, Secretary of the Interior James Harlan signed an agreement with Vinnie Ream, the humble postal worker, for the task. Vinnie's sympathetic plaster head of the martyred President had borne rich results.

Mrs. Swisshelm cattily declared in Missouri's Liberty *Tribune*, September 14,

> Miss Minie (sic) Ream who received the $10,000 for a Lincoln statue, is a young girl of about twenty who has been studying art for a few months, never made a statue, has some plaster busts on exhibition, including her own . . . has a pretty face, long dark curls and plenty of them, wears a jockey hat and a good deal of jewelry, sees members at their lodgings or in the reception room at the Capitol, urges her claims fluently and confidently, sits in the galleries in a conspicuous position and in her most bewitching dress, while those claims are being discussed on the floor, and nods and smiles as a member rises and delivers his opinion on the merits of the case with the air of a man sitting for his picture, and so she carries the day over Powers, Crawford and Hosmer, and who not?

It is little wonder that Mrs. Lincoln, influenced by her friend Mrs. Swisshelm, behaved the way she did to Vinnie Ream.

Vinnie, out of courtesy and respect, solicited the widow's help in securing a faithful likeness of the late President. Mrs. Lincoln refused even to remember her.

Chicago,
Sept. 10th 66.

Miss Vinnie Ream,

Your letter has been received and I hasten to return an early reply. I shall be unable to comply with your request and you will allow me to say you are undertaking a very sacred work, one of great responsibility, which artists of world-wide renown would shrink from, as incapable of the great task. Every man, woman and child in our land felt as if they knew my beloved and illustrious husband, even if they had seen him but once. In *your* case, your home was far removed from ours in Washington, even *if* you visited there, during the late President's administration. With his life of toil, he had no opportunities and *far* less inclination, to cultivate the acquaintance of any save those who were compelled to be with him daily in saving our great nation from the hands of its enemies.

As every friend my husband knew was familiar to me, and as your name was not on the list, consequently you could not have become familiar with the expression of his face, which was so variable, even to those and especially to myself, who had passed almost a life time in studying its changes. The photographs that abound in the country have never done justice to my dear husband, yet I will admit, if you had *even* been introduced to him in the gaping crowd, the kind and beautiful expression of his countenance would never have been forgotten.

That happiness was mine for long years of greater felicity, than is usually allotted to frail humanity and his expression was so changing, yet always so kind and almost heavenly—that with my heart *then as now*, filled with unutterable love for him who so truly and fervently returned it—I cannot fix my distressed mind—on any particular look, hence the difficulty of the task for *you*, a stranger to this great, good and Christ-like man.

Praying that you may have success,
I remain,
Truly,
MARY TODD LINCOLN

A strange letter, yet Vinnie's statue was, from its honored place in the nation's Capitol, destined to bring pleasure to succeeding generations of Americans. Neither did the matter end with the letter of Miss Vinnie Ream. During the following spring Mrs.

The Exile : : *page 173*

Lincoln wrote Alphonse Donn, a White House guard to whom she had given the clothes worn by the President on the night of his assassination.

Chicago, March 18th.

Mr. Donn,

 Mrs. Welles writes to my son Robert in regard to the suit of clothes I gave you—and which have been in the possession of Mr. Wilson the artist. She desires them for a Miss Vinnie Ream, an unknown person, who by much forwardness and unladylike persistence, obtained from Congress permission to execute a statue of my husband, the late President. From her inexperience, I judge she will be unable to do this, in a faithful manner.

 For your devoted attentions to President Lincoln, I gave you those clothes, and, after the loan you have made of them—without you see proper, you need not let them go farther. Retain them always, in memory of the best and noblest man that ever lived.

 You will understand me, when I say that it is now time for you to claim them, and you need feel under no obligations to allow them to pass out of your possession, at this time. Let me hear from you on this subject when you receive this letter—and show this letter to no one —only burn it. I feel I gave them to you I can dictate a little about them. Write a receipt of this. What you say will not be mentioned—as I remain your friend.

MRS. LINCOLN.

Use your own discretion about lending the clothes but as they are a gift from me you are under no obligations to yield them into other hands. All this you will understand. I do not wish my name mentioned in it. Write me all about it.

 Burn this and mention contents to no one.

April 2d ———67.

Mr. A. Donn———

 I write you in haste, merely to say—that you can act as

you please in the matter. This Miss Ream is an entire stranger to me and mine—and I expect is very inexperienced in her work. I trust very sincerely, she may succeed.

I remain your friend

MRS. A. LINCOLN.

[These letters came to light when in 1968 the clothing given to Donn was purchased from his descendant, Mrs. J. Marvin Smith, to go on display in the newly restored Ford's Theater, Washington, D. C.]

Mary Lincoln's letters were often written in a hurry and regretted as soon as she had mailed them.

Number 375 West Washington Street, Chicago, the house she had purchased with the Congressional grant, had brought her little pleasure, and in September she wrote a friend that even by practicing the most rigid economy she was unable to continue housekeeping on her present means. At the same time she stressed the fact that she so wanted a home in which to retire with her grief.

She was still worried over the ever-present debts that were still unpaid. Suddenly the idea formed in her clouded mind that she could sell some of the expensive jewels and clothes that were the real culprits. For a year previously she had, incognito, been pawning belongings.

Even in the White House days Mrs. Lincoln had believed that her jewels and clothing might one day prove an insurance against want. Immediately she sat down and wrote the ever-faithful Mrs. Keckley to help her. They would meet in New York, the only place where such a market was available.

Arriving on September 16 from Chicago, the heavily veiled Mrs. Lincoln registered as "Mrs. Clarke" at the St. Denis Hotel on Broadway. She had neglected to give Mrs. Keckley proper directions where to find her and in desperation sent a letter to Washington.

My dear Lizzie:

I arrived *here* last evening in utter despair at not

finding you. I am frightened to death, being here alone. Come, I pray you, by next train. Inquire for
>> Mrs. Clarke,
>> Room 94, 5th or 6th Story

When they did meet Mrs. Lincoln had harsh words with the hotel clerk who was "exquisitely arrayed, highly perfumed, and too self-important to be obliging, or even courteous."

Because of her race, he refused Mrs. Keckley a room on the same floor as Mrs. Lincoln. As a further insult she was then barred from the main dining room, being told that she must take her dinner in the servants' hall. Mrs. Keckley went without her supper; Mrs. Lincoln could not sleep for indignation.

Next morning they ate breakfast together away from the segregated dining room before proceeding to the firm of W. H. Brady & Company. When a Mr. Keyes found Mrs. Lincoln's real name upon a ring the secret of her identity was revealed. Hastily she left the premises.

Brady and Keyes, knowing well the advertising potential for their firm, soon called upon her, promising that if she would leave her affairs in their hands they would net her "at least $100,000 in a few weeks." While the negotiations were proceeding, the two women tried their hand at selling some of the clothing but met with little success.

Mrs. Lincoln was persuaded by Brady and Keyes to write certain letters that they might show to prominent politicians. These explained why Brady's firm was selling her things because she was "pressed in a most startling manner for means of common subsistence. . . . that men of the Republican party for whom my noble husband did so much . . . unhesitatingly deprived me of all means of support and left me in a pitiless condition." Mrs. Keckley says, "Mr. Brady proposed to show the letters to certain politicians, and ask for money on a threat to publish them if his demands, as Mrs. Lincoln's agent, were not complied with." The scheme fell through, leaving Mrs. Lincoln with a commission bill of eight hundred dollars payable to the Brady firm.

When Brady published her personal letters in the New York *World*, Mrs. Lincoln was horrified. Home in Chicago, the letters scandal followed when they were reprinted in a local newspaper.

Her anguish is apparent in a letter written to Mrs. Keckley on October 6.

> I am writing this morning with a broken heart after a sleepless night of great mental suffering. R[obert] came up last evening like a maniac, and almost threatening his life, looking like death, because the letters of the *World* were published in yesterday's paper. . . . I pray for death this morning. Only my darling Taddie prevents my taking my life. . . . Tell Mr. Brady and Keyes not to have a line of mine once more in print. I am nearly losing my reason."

The Old-Clothes Scandal was now aired in the nation's press, some newspapers hinting that the former First Lady was blackmailing politicians who had taken part in dishonest transactions of which she was aware. A new smear campaign originated. In order to gain time to pack up the nation's treasures, "she had pretended to be an expectant mother" they said, "to prolong her White House sojourn after the President's death." Richmond's *Southern Opinion* thought she was contemplating matrimony again. It also published a hateful parody.

> What Cabinet member (now hid in the dark)
> Bought his seat by gifts to you, fair Mrs. Clarke?
> What opulent presents were made in advance
> By seekers of missions to Russia and France?

Early in 1868 she was still trying to get her ill-fated clothes out of the hands of the odious Mr. Brady. When she heard that some of Lincoln's personal belongings she had given Mrs. Keckley might be exhibited in Europe she wrote that "R[obert] would go *raving distracted* if such a thing was done." The painful memory of the curious flocking to the Brady establishment to examine her own things was still too fresh.

When in the spring of 1868 Mrs. Keckley published a small book entitled *Behind the Scenes,* describing life in the White

House, Mrs. Lincoln never forgave her. Mrs. Keckley's inoffensive book was accurate, and she actually thought she was helping Mrs. Lincoln by writing it. So ended the relationship between Mary Todd Lincoln and one of the few people she could trust.

In spite of all the clothing furor, the debts did get paid, it was believed, by certain Republican politicians. At last she could write: "It is my comfort to know, that I do not owe, a dollar in the world."

Mary continued to pour out her innermost thoughts in letters, many of which have survived. With the exception of her dealings with money and her fear of penury, her mind seems to have been otherwise normal. Even Robert conceded that ". . . it is very hard to deal with one who is sane on all subjects but one."

She could write as kindly to some as she had written unkindly to Vinnie Ream. A blind girl who had sent a message of sympathy touched her deeply. She wrote in reply,

> My dear young friend,
> Although unknown to me, I love you, for being able, so thoroughly to appreciate the noble character of my idolized husband. . . . My . . . husband, was the *light* of our eyes—we never felt . . . that we could love him sufficiently . . . life is *all darkness*, the sun is a mockery to me, in my great sorrow.

To the people of France she wrote a magnificent letter thanking them for the gold medal they sent her. In it she mentioned her late husband's role in world democracy. To his much-loved stepmother she wrote a tender letter promising to help her if she was in need.

She thought of sending Tad to boarding school at Racine, Wisconsin, but a visit to the institution displeased her so she decided otherwise. "There was an air of *restraint* which I did not exactly like," she confessed, and she was shocked by the sight of "the little white cots of the boys."

Following Robert's wedding to Mary Harlan, Mary and Tad set sail October 1 on the *City of Baltimore* for Germany. To Mrs.

A Rose for Mrs. Lincoln : : page 178

Orne she gives her reasons that to avoid "persecution, from the vampyre press . . . I had to flee to a land of strangers for refuge."

At Frankfurt-am-Main she enrolled Tad in the "Institute" of Dr. Hohagen where she tells us he studied "with a number of well behaved German and English boys." A former army chaplain, F. W. Bogen noted aboard ship the "quiet and throughout dignified deportment" of Mrs. Lincoln. Writing Charles Sumner later, he tells of her life in Frankfurt:

> She lives very retiredly in the Hotel d'Angleterre, occupies only one room, sees few friends, yet her daily necessary Hotel expenses (she takes her meals in her room, in order not to be exposed to the gaze of the curious) are nearly 9 florins, the lowest rate at which she could reduce them. To Bogen she explained that because she was a President's widow, and the mistaken thought that the American government was giving her a large pension, she was overcharged.

Her hopes for such a pension did not decrease.

During Tad's summer holidays in 1869, mother and son visited Scotland where, for a brief period, Mary knew a measure of happiness. Traveling incognito, the name of Mrs. Lincoln was not spoken during their seven weeks' stay. They visited the birthplace of Robert Burns, and also her former pastor, the Reverend James Smith.

Back in her one room in Frankfurt, the former First Lady was visited by the sympathetic and understanding Mrs. Orne, who calling upon her friend one evening was so shocked with what she found that she immediately wrote Charles Sumner.

> I followed the waiter to the *fourth story* and the back part of it too—and there in a small cheerless desolate looking room with but one window—two chairs and a wooden table with a solitary candle—I found *the wife the petted indulged wife* of my *noble* hearted just good *murdered* President Abraham Lincoln—the "Justinian"—can you believe it? It would be hard to say which overcame me most

the painful meeting or *the place*—My very blood boiled within my veins and I almost *cried out—shame on my countrymen*—Mrs. Lincoln was completely overwhelmed with grief—her sobs and tears wrung my own heart and I thought at the moment if her *tormentors* and *slanderers* could see her—they surely *might be satisfied.*

Mrs. Orne was horrified to discover there was a rumor current that Mrs. Lincoln had assisted in the assassination of her husband, so that even the hotel servants treated her with rudeness. "*To say she lives retired,*" said Mrs. Orne, "does not express her manner of life—she lives *alone*. I never knew what the word *Alone* meant before."

Mrs. Orne was eager to acquaint Senator Sumner with the grim facts of Mrs. Lincoln's present status, for he was fighting to get her a pension. A bill was introduced in the Senate on January 14, 1869, to provide Mrs. Lincoln with a lifetime pension, the amount left blank. In February a letter from her was read in the Senate when Senator Sumner proposed an annual amount of $5,000. Unfortunately, the Fortieth Congress did not pass the bill. Undaunted, Senator Sumner introduced another bill on March 5, 1869, again asking for $5,000 a year. There was much opposition; all the old rumors were revived concerning the unfortunate woman. Anxiously she awaited news of the bill's progress. Going to an English reading room in Frankfurt during May she met what she described to Mrs. Orne as "*my terrible fate.*" One of the English newspapers related that the Senate committee had decided against her pension because she owned property amounting to $60,000.

Mrs. Lincoln collapsed and a doctor was called. Twelve hours later she left for Bohemia where she took a third-floor room. She longed to die.

The fight went on. Simon Cameron spoke out on her behalf. She was, he insisted, the victim of slander; that Lincoln's enemies had succeeded in giving her a bad reputation. Even her husband's so-called friends made vicious attacks, like Richard Yates of Illinois who even questioned her faithfulness. "A woman should be true to her husband," he thundered, without giving details to justify so terrible an accusation.

A Rose for Mrs. Lincoln : : *page 180*

It was not until July 14, 1870, over five years after Lincoln's death, that a pension of $3,000 a year was granted his widow. Ironically, less than half the Republican senators voted for its passage.

That September, Mary and Tad were in England in order to escape the Franco-Prussian war. She found an English tutor for her son, "very highly educated—very quiet and gentlemanly and patience itself."

Of Mrs. Lincoln, an Englishman noted, "I could not for the life of me recognize the Mrs. Lincoln of the newspapers in the Mrs. Lincoln I saw." He described her as being bright, sympathetic, cordial and sensible "with no trace of eccentricity in conduct or manner." Mrs. Orne found the same qualities evident in her friend. Writing the faithful Charles Sumner, she says: "I have watched her closely—by day and by night—for weeks—and fail to discover any evidence of aberration of mind in her."

The critical Benjamin Moran of the American Legation in London confided his description of meeting with "the wife of the ex-President Lincoln" on September 4, 1870, and of being "agreeably surprised to find her an unpretending woman of excellent manners, much intelligence and very lady like appearance." She was dressed all in black with a widow's cap. "I am prepared to believe that all the attacks upon her in the newspapers were sheer scandal and falsehoods," he insisted. Her "very decided Southern accent" was much in evidence.

Suffering with painful rheumatism and a hacking cough, she left for Italy early in 1871, leaving Tad in an English school. In the Spring they returned to America, excited at the prospect of seeing Robert's baby daughter, born the previous autumn and, to the delight of the new grandmother, also named Mary. "Little Mamie" they called her.

At last in Chicago, Mary Lincoln held the precious baby in her arms. She was fond of her daughter-in-law, having made a habit of sending her small gifts from Europe. "I never see anything particularly pretty that I do not wish it was yours," she wrote Mary Harlan Lincoln.

CHAPTER TWENTY

TAD

Tad was delighted with his new niece. Life had not treated him kindly, for it was he who had borne the brunt of all his unfortunate mother's illnesses and depressions. Whenever she was sick it was Tad who was there to nurse and take care of her. Mrs. Orne noted when she had seen him in Germany how much he resembled his father in looks and ways. His mother saw the likeness too. She had seen the same tender look in Abraham's eyes.

Robert was much impressed by the way that Tad had overcome his serious speech defect by reading aloud in Germany. He now spoke English with a slight German accent. Robert spoke of his "articulating perfectly, but with deliberation."

The New York *Tribune* gives this description of Tad upon his return from Europe.

> He has grown up a tall, fine-looking lad of 18, who bears but
> a faint resemblance to the tricksy little sprite whom
> visitors to the White House remember.

He was not strong however. Long hours of study in Germany and England, in addition to the exhausting times he had spent pacifying his mother in her many declines had played havoc with his own health. He was probably tubercular. Like his father, he could always appeal to his mother's better nature by compliments and affection. "My mother is a great woman," he would tell her. Once she even left off her mourning for his birthday.

Just after mother and son arrived in Chicago Tad developed a bad cold. His condition worsened and then improved. On June 8 his mother wrote Mrs. Albert S. White, a member of the noted Randolph family of Virginia, "My dear boy has been *very, very* dangerously ill. . . . I have been sitting up . . . constantly for the last ten nights."

Due to a form of dropsy in the chest, for six weeks the invalid could only sit in a chair. Robert was grieved at "such suffering." It was now Mary's turn to minister to Tad and she did so devotedly. By the second week in July there seemed at last some improvement in the patient. Robert was able to joke with his one remaining brother, and to bring him a picture of little Mamie at which he gazed with much pleasure.

Next morning at 4:30 Robert was aroused to hear that his brother had suffered a relapse. After several hours of watching Tad's suffering, Mary saw him topple forward in his chair. Again she had lost a son.

Once more there was a journey to Springfield that had to be undertaken without her. Prostrate with grief she lay again in a darkened room, not caring whether she lived or died. Tad was laid to rest beside his father, leaving his mother to write, "One by one I have consigned to their resting place, my idolized ones, and now, in *this* world, there is nothing left me, but the deepest anguish and desolation."

With Tad gone his mother had become a bundle of nerves unable to concentrate upon the future. Robert engaged Mrs. Richard Fitzgerald, mother of Eddie Foy the actor, as traveling companion, nurse and guard. She seemed unable to settle anywhere. A dropsical condition which she called "bloating" sent her to Wisconsin in the summer of 1872 to take advantage of the medicinal waters. Everywhere she went the public followed; there was little privacy. Besides, at the end of May a sensational *Life of Abraham Lincoln* by Ward H. Lamon was published, causing another furor of gossip that brought his widow further humiliation.

Herndon, being in financial difficulties due to drink and the neglect of his law practice, had sold copies of his own Lincoln material to Lamon, who in turn engaged Chauncey Black, a man who detested Lincoln, to ghost-write the book. Not only was the Ann Rutledge story resurrected but also the rumors that Lincoln was illegitimate and not even a Christian. Again his marriage with Mary Todd was declared an unhappy one.

Once more the widow issued denials, embroiling herself in a public quarrel with Herndon who, lecturing in Springfield December 12, 1873, had called Lincoln an infidel. Again he quoted Mary as saying during their fateful interview of 1866 that her husband was not a "technical Christian."

In the *Illinois State Journal* for December 10, 1873, a front page story declared that Mrs. Lincoln "denies unequivocally that she had the conversation with Mr. Herndon, as stated by him." This last phrase "as stated by him" was misinterpreted by both the reading public and Herndon, who thought that Mrs. Lincoln was denying she had ever given the interview. When the story was picked up by the nation's press Herndon was mortified. Now his hate for Lincoln's widow knew no bounds. Immediately he released verbal venom upon the unfortunate woman, branding her a liar subjected to "spasmodic madness."

Writing her cousin, John Todd Stuart, Mary instructed him not to deny that she had been interviewed by Herndon. All she denied was the false way in which he had presented her statements. "Entirely perverted" and "utterly false" were the words she used.

Lamon's book was the first publication to put into print the insinuation that Lincoln was illegitimate, which infuriated Robert as much as it hurt his mother. Fearing that their surname might in truth be "Hanks" instead of "Lincoln," Robert sought information concerning the marriage of Thomas Lincoln and Nancy Hanks. Abraham himself had inserted the date of his parents' marriage in the family Bible. After Lincoln had been murdered, Dennis Hanks had torn out the page, folding it, so that by the time Herndon saw it there were only torn fragments left. The all-important marriage date was missing, causing Herndon to form his damaging conclusion of Lincoln's illegitimacy. What he did not know was that another of the relatives had made a full record of the page before it had been detached from the Bible. Robert had a copy made of this, which Mary spoke of in a letter to her cousin John. "The *missing*

A Rose for Mrs. Lincoln : : page 184

page—which you know will *once more safe and sure* make us Lincoln's *once more* . . . is deposited in my son's vault."

Here, unfortunately, the matter did not end, for a gullible public, caring little about Herndon's flimsy "research" and incredible conclusions, still gossiped over the supposed illegitimacy. Unable to stop Herndon's tongue or Lamon's pen, Lincoln's widow underwent further tortures of frustration.

In March of 1875 she was in Florida, suffering from delusions of persecution, which is understandable in the light of the years of persecution she had actually endured. Now she lived in fear of the unknown, leaving the gaslight on in her room all night, pacing the floor in her loneliness with one eye always upon the window, fearful of what nameless horror lurked outside.

She was frightened to eat in case her food was poisoned; once, upon entering a public eating place, she was heard to murmur, "I am afraid; I am afraid." Even her dress had lost its neat appearance; she was plagued with the hallucination that Robert, her one remaining son, was ill. On March 12 she telegraphed Robert's doctor in Chicago. "My belief is my son is ill; telegraph. I start for Chicago tomorrow." The doctor contacted Robert who was in good health. Immediately he telegraphed his mother, suggesting she stay in Florida, but she had already sent him another message. "My dearly beloved son, Robert T. Lincoln—Rouse yourself and live for your mother; you are all I have; from this hour all I have is yours. I pray every night that you may be spared to your mother."

Upon arriving in Chicago she went to the Grand Pacific Hotel, where Robert found her with fifty thousand dollars on her person. She would not go to his home so he stayed in an adjoining room at the hotel, getting little sleep because of her terrible fears that came with the darkness. When she left her room improperly dressed, Robert and a member of the hotel staff tried to get her back inside, while she screamed, "You are going to murder me."

Robert was frightened that his mother would cash her securities and spend them. She still liked to shop, making friends with the shopkeepers and their assistants, who seemed to supply the affection she craved. Her last shopping spree was to buy eight pairs of lace curtains on the morning of Tuesday, May 19, 1875. These were duly delivered by a boy to Mrs. Lincoln in her hotel room at

Robert Lincoln. *From the collections of the Library of Congress.*

A Rose for Mrs. Lincoln : : page 186

1:00 P.M. He was not alone, for also waiting at the door were Leonard T. Swett, a Chicago lawyer who had helped Lincoln to secure the 1860 Presidential nomination, and Samuel M. Turner, the manager of the hotel. The boy left the packages and disappeared. Mrs. Lincoln, unusually cheerful, seemed pleased to see her husband's old friend, Swett, and invited him in. The lawyer immediately informed her that she was under arrest.

Turner could stand no more, and left the room. Mrs. Lincoln was surprisingly calm. What were the charges, she demanded with the air of a queen, only to be told that Robert had asked for an insanity hearing. Mrs. Lincoln called the charge preposterous. Who had decided she was insane, she asked. Swett produced letters from five physicians, adding that Judge David Davis who had served as conservator of her husband's estate, believed her to be crazy. Either she accompanied him peacefully to the court or, as an alternative, downstairs two officers of the law were waiting.

The two continued to argue, she being firm in her denouncement of Swett, Judge Davis, and her son; yet Swett himself later testified that the former First Lady used no common words or phrases. It was a court order, Swett insisted; it would be useless to resist. He refused to leave the room so that she might change her clothing, but this she was finally able to do by stepping into a small closet. Outside, a carriage waited to take them both to the Cook County Criminal Court and county jail building located at West Hubbard and North Dearborn Streets.

A second carriage followed carrying the two law enforcement officers, the hotel manager Turner, and Ben Ayer, serving with Swett as counsel for Robert Lincoln. It was almost 3:00 P.M. when the strange party reached the courtroom.

There the hapless woman was confronted by a ready-selected jury—most of them personal friends of Robert's, who had been sworn and waiting for an hour. Word was getting abroad; the courtroom was filling with spectators. Mrs. Lincoln recoiled at the sight.

With quiet dignity she listened while no less than seventeen witnesses, assembled by Robert, had their say. The court was petitioned to allow Robert Lincoln to take over his mother's estate and to commit her to an asylum for the insane. The jury granted

Robert his wishes, returning a verdict of insanity. The trial was in fact a mockery, for Mrs. Lincoln had been given no time properly to select her own defense attorney. Isaac N. Arnold, another "old friend" of her husband's, had been conveniently present to defend her. Even he considered his new client insane.

The statutory right to participate in the selection of a jury and the exercising of peremptory challenges deemed to be in her best interests had likewise been denied Mary Todd Lincoln in what was little more than a kangaroo court.

The name of President Lincoln's widow was inserted on page 596 of the "Lunatic Record" of the Cook County Court. The statement, "Does not manifest homicidal or suicidal tendencies," was written in, while the information "free from vermin or any infectious disease" was crossed out. Mary Todd Lincoln was ordered "committed to a State hospital for the Insane."

Robert was weeping as he went to his mother and took her hand. "O Robert," she reproached him, still half unbelievingly, "to think that my son would ever have done this." She said no more. Her last public appearance was over.

She was returned to the hotel with attendants to guard her. They proved negligent for she was able to elude them to visit several drugstores, searching for camphor and laudanum. She had weathered all her many sorrows without attempting to end her life, yet Robert's betrayal was more than she could bear. At last one druggist sold her a harmless mixture bearing the label she sought. She drank it expecting death. Next morning she awoke, to be conveyed to Bellevue Place, Batavia, Illinois, a private sanatorium superintended by Dr. R. J. Patterson.

News of Mrs. Lincoln's "trial" and committal traveled across the land. Mrs. Orne was so upset that she immediately wrote Robert asking pertinent questions. Robert's reply was full of explanations of how he felt it his duty to put his mother away. She was in the private part of the sanatorium, where she could even walk, talk, and eat with members of Dr. Patterson's own family. A carriage was at her disposal; she could receive calls and return them if accompanied by a responsible person.

"We are on the best of terms," he tried to reassure the well-meaning Mrs. Orne. "So far as I can see she does not realize her situation at all." How wrong he was. His mother was not going to confide in the son who had caused her incarceration. For the first time in her life she was having competent medical treatment for her hysteria, a treatment that was so successful that we do not hear of the problem again. Instead of being like a ship without a rudder, having no purpose in life, she had one consuming ambition—to regain her lost liberty. Sensibly she enlisted the friendly help of Judge and Mrs. James B. Bradwell whom she had known in the past. Mrs. Bradwell had the distinction of being the first woman lawyer in Illinois. These two intelligent people were convinced that not only was Mrs. Lincoln sane but that she had been cruelly wronged. Wrote Mrs. Lincoln,

> When all others, among them my husband's supposed friends, failed me in the most bitter hours of my life, those loyal hearts, Myra Bradwell and her husband, came to my assistance and rescued me, and under great difficulty secured my release from confinement in an insane asylum.

Dr. Patterson was so upset by stories that his most famous patient was "locked by her jailer as a prisoner," that he aired his own feelings in a public letter. He was indignant at Judge Bradwell's writing him "a threatening and insulting letter" in which he called himself Mrs. Lincoln's "legal adviser and friend."

Not only were the Bradwells standing behind Mary Lincoln, but so were her sister and brother-in-law, Elizabeth and Ninian Edwards. In an age when the word "lunatic" was interpreted as being on a par with "criminal," they were furious that Robert should have brought such personal disgrace upon the family.

So adamant did they become that Dr. Patterson was unable to stop them from moving Mary, after four months' "imprisonment" to their Springfield home, where she had married Abraham so long ago. Mary still bore the stigma of an insane person, and another nine months passed before she was granted a second sanity hearing which took place in Chicago on June 15, 1876. At that time a proper jury decided that "the said Mary Lincoln is restored to reason and is capable to manage and control her estate."

Mary traveled back to Springfield, where on June 19 she wrote Robert a stinging letter. "Robert T. Lincoln," it began and, coming as it did from one who had always been the most endearing of mothers, this alone cut him to the quick. "I am now in constant receipt of letters, from my friends denouncing you in the bitterest terms, six letters from prominent, *respectable* Chicago people such as you do not associate with." She told him that two ministers had even offered to pray for him that he might be forgiven for the wicked way he had treated his sick mother. Mary then demanded he return all her possessions which she listed in careful detail. "Send me all that I have written for," she ordered him, "you have tried your game of robbery long enough."

Recalling his indignant aunt, Mrs. Edwards, she continues, "Trust not to the belief, that Mrs. Edwards's tongue, has not been *rancorous* against you all winter and she has maintained to the very last, that you dared not venture into her house and our presence."

For years afterwards Robert Lincoln tried to recover letters that his mother wrote to various people during this sad period of estrangement which, he insisted, showed "the distressing mental disorder of my mother."

The Edwardses were kindness itself to Mary. Any past ill-will between the two sisters was completely forgotten, Mary filling her letters to relatives and friends with gratitude for their devotion. She no longer held any affection for her once-beloved cousin John Todd Stuart, for she had been told that he had advised Robert to hold the infamous insanity trial.

Then into Mary's barren life came a charming and brilliant young man who so reminded her, she said, of her own lost Willie and Tad. Edward Lewis Baker, Jr., was Mrs. Edwards's grandson, then about seventeen years old. With Robert cast from her affections, Mary again felt wanted when Lewis gave her small attentions and "a sweet affection."

During the summer of 1861 she had sent Lewis's mother a bottle of precious water from the River Jordan, that he might be christened with it. Now she told him, "Love crowned you at your birth."

Yet even Lewis's love and his grandparents' understanding

could not protect her from that terrible stigma of insanity. At times Mary became so ashamed that she once told her sister, "I cannot endure to meet my former friends, Lizzie; they will never cease to regard me as a lunatic, I feel it in their soothing manner. If I should say the moon is made of green cheese they would heartily and smilingly agree with me. I love you, but I cannot stay. I would be much less unhappy in the midst of strangers."

So with Lewis accompanying her as far as New York, the President's lonely widow once more set out for "an exile" in France. For four years she would write her beloved Lewis regularly, telling him of all she was doing.

At the port of Le Havre on October 17, 1876, she was deeply touched by the attention and care showered upon her by the inhabitants. She promised Lewis that in future she would behave in a more "civilized manner" and not keep herself in such seclusion from the world.

She did not write the unfortunate Robert; indeed by his own admission he did not even know where in Europe his mother was staying, but to Lewis she wrote glowingly, "*Words*, are impossible to express, *how* near you are to my heart." She begged Lewis to travel, suggesting places he must see that in a happier past had given her pleasure. Lewis, suddenly losing his two small sisters, turned to his great-aunt for comfort. "We are never prepared for these things," she told him—and she of all people should have known. "God, gives us our beloved ones, we make them our idols, they are removed from us and we have patiently to await the time, when *He* reunites us to them. And the *waiting*, is so long!"

She had left her financial affairs in the capable hands of Jacob Bunn of Springfield. Eighty-nine business letters are in existence written him during her "exile." Carefully she watched the fluctuations of gold, and discussed the difficulties of exchange and interest through living abroad. Certainly no woman bereft of her senses wrote these letters.

Then one day in June, 1879, she was reading the *American Register* published in Paris and came across the startling suggestion that her only surviving son, Robert, would make a good candidate for the Presidency. Once more she was the bubbling, excitable

Mary of her youth. Abraham's son in the White House. Little Mamie, her beloved granddaughter growing up within those historic walls. She even began to consider whom Robert might have in his Cabinet! For a few moments all the bitterness was gone and she was Robert's affectionate mother again.

She did not really enjoy her exile, missing especially her lifelong love, the American political scene. She was most indignant when President Rutherford B. Hayes had the audacity to place David M. Key in his Cabinet. The former First Lady scathingly described Key as "a man who served in the Confederate Army, during the War. We have too many other men in our Country, with talents and patriotism, to the *true cause*, not to reward a Secessionist."

This well-born Southern lady was still just as loyal to her husband's ideals as she had been during those days in the White House when that loyalty had been so cruelly questioned.

She was living in Pau, a health resort, for now her health was visibly failing. The rheumatism that had plagued her for years was especially painful. She continually contracted boils; her eyesight was failing. Matters came to a head in December, 1879, when, attempting to hang a picture over a mantlepiece, she fell from the stepladder, badly hurting her spine. This injury resulted in partial paralysis of the lower part of her body. The pain was excessive; in mid-January she weighed only a hundred pounds. Now she knew the time had come to go home.

To Lewis she wrote a pathetic letter, begging him to meet her when the steamer docked in New York. She sailed on *L'Amérique* on October 16. Also aboard was the famed actress, Sarah Bernhardt, who, writing in *Memories of My Life*, tells of how she noticed on deck "a lady dressed in black with a sad, resigned face." Suddenly the steamer lurched so that both women were thrown forward, but Sarah's seizing of the other woman's skirts saved her from falling down a stairway.

The lady in black, hurt though she was, thanked the actress in a "gentle, dreamy voice."

"You might have been killed, madame, down that horrible staircase," sympathized the actress.

A Rose for Mrs. Lincoln : : page 192

"Yes," said the other woman with an audible sigh, "but it was not God's will."

Then Sarah Bernhardt revealed her own identity to which the lady in black replied, "I am the widow of President Lincoln." The actress was stunned. "I had just done this unhappy woman the only service that I ought not to have done her—I had saved her from death."

Faithful Lewis was on the dock when the steamer arrived and, with his sick and aging great-aunt, was jostled and pushed back into the excited crowd waiting to welcome the great Bernhardt to America. Mary instructed Lewis to register them at their hotel as "Edward Lewis Baker and Aunt."

Together they traveled back to his grandparents' home in Springfield. Elizabeth was waiting with open arms. Robert came to visit his mother in May of 1881, to ask her forgiveness. He brought little Mamie with him. Even so he could not comprehend just how ill his mother was. Writing the faithful Mrs. Orne he says rather callously, "The reports you have seen about her are exaggerated very much. She is undoubtedly far from well and has not been out of her room for more than six months and she thinks she is very ill. My own judgment is that some part of her trouble is imaginary."

Mary was in so much pain by the fall of 1881 that she made the long journey to New York City to obtain the advice of Dr. Lewis A. Sayre, a brilliant orthopedic surgeon who is said to have met her years before when they were both young people in Kentucky. She was staying at Dr. E. P. Miller's medical baths on West 26th Street, where, in November, a newspaper reporter found her unable to move without assistance because of her old spinal injury.

"She is, in fact, deserted and next to friendless with the exception of her son Robert and his wife, Mary, who visit her at intervals of two or three weeks," he wrote. He also added significantly, "Mentally Mrs. Lincoln is active and clear, talks with great rapidity, and is pleased to meet her friends who may call to visit her."

When Mr. and Mrs. N. W. Miner saw her they complained of the poorly furnished room in which she lay on a sofa propped up with pillows, finding her "almost blind," "gray-haired," "partially paralyzed," with nobody to wait upon her.

Mr. Miner was so incensed that before a pastors' conference he gave a passionate address vindicating Mrs. Lincoln. So much national publicity did this receive that in January, 1882, even Congress was moved to increase her pension from $3,000 to $5,000 annually, in addition to donating her the sum of $15,000. Even so, Mr. Miner's kindness had also revived many of the old untrue stories about her, and she asked him,

> Mr. Miner, what have I done, that I am so persecuted by the press? I am a poor, lonely woman; my husband is dead, and three of my sons are dead; my health is shattered, and I am almost blind from constant weeping. I try to keep myself secluded from the world, but I cannot escape them; they will follow me, and say hard and cruel things about me. I long to leave the world and be at rest.

Lewis received his last letter from New York dated March 21, 1882, in which, in the handwriting grown large and uneven, she asks him to meet her upon arriving in Springfield. The invalid chair was going on ahead; would he look out for it?

So Mary Todd Lincoln returned finally to the house where she had married Abraham. Her room was darkened; only dim candles burned for no longer could her poor, tortured eyes bear the light of day. She told one kind soul who was looking after her that the empty space on the large bed was "the President's place." At the end the memory of the only man she had ever loved was there close beside her.

The heat of July found her sufferings increased by a painful attack of boils. It was a Saturday when, with help, she managed to walk for the last time across the shaded room. That evening her body became quite paralyzed and she lapsed into a merciful unconsciousness. She died quietly on Sunday evening, July 16, 1882.

They buried her beside the President in Oak Ridge Cemetery with all the proper dignity befitting the widow of so great a man. The residents of Springfield sent a floral book made of carnations with the words MARY LINCOLN written in blue forget-me-nots.

The Reverend James A. Reed, in the oration he preached during the funeral service in the First Presbyterian Church, dwelt particularly upon the symbolical story of two straight pine trees growing together on a hill, their roots and branches intertwined. Then a storm came and lightning struck down one of the pines, leaving the other alone and apparently unhurt. "Its after-subsistence was merely a living death," he told the mourners. "Similar was the course of life with the illustrious Lincoln and his mate."

It was, however, Jane Grey Swisshelm, the writer, who was left to pen a final epitaph for the woman who now lay in death still with the ring inscribed "Love is Eternal" upon her marriage finger. Said Mrs. Swisshelm,

> I want to write of her as a historical character—as one to whom the people of this country owe a great reparation,
> but can only think of her as a most affectionate, faithful friend.

SELECTED BIBLIOGRAPHY

BEVERIDGE, ALBERT J., *Abraham Lincoln—1809–1858*, 2 vols. (Boston and New York: Houghton Mifflin Company, 1928).

BRADFORD, GAMALIEL, *Wives* (New York: Harper & Brothers, 1925).

DRINKWATER, JOHN, *Abraham Lincoln—A Play*, with an introduction by Arnold Bennett (Boston: Houghton Mifflin Company, 1919).

EVANS, W. A., *Mrs. Abraham Lincoln—A Study of Her Personality and Her Influence on Lincoln* (New York: Alfred A. Knopf, 1932).

FURMAN, BESS, *White House Profile* (Indianapolis and New York: The Bobbs-Merrill Company, Inc., 1951).

GRIMSLEY, ELIZABETH TODD, "Six Months in the White House," article by Mrs. Lincoln's bridesmaid in the *Journal of the Illinois State Historical Society,* Vol. XIX, October 1926–January 1927.

HALL, GORDON LANGLEY, *Vinnie Ream—The Story of the Girl Who Sculptured Lincoln* (New York: Holt, Rinehart and Winston, 1963).

HANAFORD, PHEBE A., *Daughters of America* (Augusta, Maine: True and Company, 1882).

HELM, KATHERINE, *The True Story of Mary, Wife of Lincoln* (New York and London: Harper & Brothers, 1928).

Selected Bibliography : : page 196

HOPE, EVA, *Lincoln and Garfield—America's Two Hero Presidents* (New York and Melbourne, Newcastle-on-Tyne, England, 1924).

JEFFERSON, JOSEPH, *Rip Van Winkle*, an autobiography, with a foreword by Eleanor Farjeon (New York: Appleton-Century-Crofts, Inc., 1949).

KINNAIRD, VIRGINIA, "Mrs. Lincoln as a White House Hostess," article in *Papers in Illinois History and Transactions for the Year 1938* (Springfield, Illinois: The Illinois State Historical Society, 1939).

LEECH, MARGARET, *Reveille in Washington 1860–1865* (New York: Harper & Brothers, 1941).

MEANS, MARIANNE, *The Woman in the White House—The Lives, Times and Influence of Twelve Notable First Ladies* (New York: Random House, 1963).

PRATT, HARRY E., and ERNEST E. EAST, "Mrs. Lincoln Refurbishes the White House," pamphlet (Harrogate, Tennessee: Department of Lincolniana, Lincoln Memory University, 1945).

PRINDIVILLE, KATHLEEN, *First Ladies—Stories of the Presidents' Wives*, with introduction by Adrienne Foulke, 2nd ed. (New York: The Macmillan Company, 1964).

RANDALL, RUTH PAINTER, *Mary Lincoln, A Biography of a Marriage* (Boston: Little, Brown and Company, 1953).

RHODES, JAMES A., and DEAN JAUCHIUS, *The Trial of Mary Todd Lincoln* (Indianapolis and New York: The Bobbs-Merrill Company, Inc., 1959).

SANDBURG, CARL, and PAUL M. ANGLE, *Mary Lincoln, Wife and Widow* (New York: Harcourt Brace and Company, 1932).

TOWNSEND, WILLIAM H., *Lincoln and His Wife's Home Town* (Indianapolis and New York: The Bobbs-Merrill Company, Inc., 1929).

———, *The Boarding School of Mary Todd Lincoln* (Lexington, Kentucky: privately printed, 1941).

———, *Lincoln and the Bluegrass—Slavery and Civil War in Kentucky* (Lexington: University of Kentucky Press, 1955).

WEFER, MARION, "Another Assassination, Another Widow,

Selected Bibliography : : *page 197*

Another Embattled Book," article in *American Heritage*, August 1967.

The White House (Washington, D.C.: The White House Historical Association, 1963).